D1523288

The Most Memorable Moments in Olympic Swimming

ROWMAN & LITTLEFIELD SWIMMING SERIES

Series Editor: John Lohn

The Rowman & Littlefield Swimming Series looks at competitive swimming from a number of perspectives, providing readers with the historical context of the events, athletes, and developments that have shaped the sport.

They Ruled the Pool: The 100 Greatest Swimmers in History, by John Lohn, 2013.
Duels in the Pool: Swimming's Greatest Rivalries, by Matthew De George, 2013.
Pooling Talent: Swimming's Greatest Teams, by Matthew De George, 2014.
The Most Memorable Moments in Olympic Swimming, by John Lohn, 2014.

The Most Memorable Moments in Olympic Swimming

John P. Lohn

ROWMAN & LITTLEFIELD
Lanham • Boulder • New York • London

Published by Rowman & Littlefield
A wholly owned subsidiary of The Rowman & Littlefield Publishing Group, Inc.
4501 Forbes Boulevard, Suite 200, Lanham, Maryland 20706
www.rowman.com

16 Carlisle Street, London W1D 3BT, United Kingdom

British Library Cataloguing in Publication Information Available

Library of Congress Cataloging-in-Publication Data Available

ISBN: 978-1-4422-3699-8 (cloth)
ISBN: 978-1-4422-3700-1 (electronic)

♾™ The paper used in this publication meets the minimum requirements of
American National Standard for Information Sciences—Permanence of Paper
for Printed Library Materials, ANSI/NISO Z39.48-1992.

Printed in the United States of America

Contents

Chronology

A Quick Look at the Best Moments in Olympic Swimming History

1. WELCOME THE WOMEN

Sixteen years after the men started racing at the Olympic Games, women's events were added to the schedule at the 1912 Games in Stockholm. Australian Fanny Durack became the first female champion, winning the 100 freestyle.

2. BEFORE HE SWUNG FROM VINES

To most people, Johnny Weissmuller was Tarzan and a star of motion pictures. Before he rose to fame for his historic yell, though, Weissmuller established himself as a legendary swimmer, winning back-to-back Olympic gold medals in the 100 freestyle at the 1924 and 1928 Games.

3. THE DAWN OF GREATNESS

At the 1964 Olympics in Tokyo, Australian Dawn Fraser made history by becoming the first swimmer—male or female—to win an event at three consecutive Olympiads, accomplishing the feat in the 100 freestyle. In the half-century that has passed since that achievement, only two other individuals have joined Fraser in that exclusive club.

4. MEYER'S GOLD MINE

More than 40 years after competing at the 1968 Games in Mexico City, the United States' Debbie Meyer remains the only individual in Olympic history to win gold medals in three freestyle events in the same Olympiad.

5. SEVEN FOR SPITZ

Before Michael Phelps became the most iconic figure in swimming history, Mark Spitz stood alone. His seven gold medals at the 1972 Olympics in Munich all arrived in world-record time.

6. HELLO AND GOODBYE

The career of Australian Shane Gould was brief, lasting just one Olympiad and not stretching beyond her teenage years. But before she left the sport, Gould won five individual medals at the 1972 Games in Munich, a feat that remains unmatched by another female. Her legacy short, it still remains powerful.

7. A MATTER OF TIMING

If the epic 400 individual medley race from the 1972 Olympics between Sweden's Gunnar Larsson and the United States' Tim McKee was held today, both men would own gold medals. Instead, Larsson is the only man who owns the pinnacle of Olympic achievement, with the timing rules of the day playing in his favor.

8. GULPING DOWN GOLD

East Germany's female athletes of the 1970s and 1980s were forced to swallow anabolic steroids to aid their performances. Due to this systematic doping program, many of their competitors were robbed of their rightful place in history, while the East German athletes were victimized by health issues and questions of how good they really were.

9. USA ALL THE WAY

At the 1976 Olympics in Montreal, the U.S. men put together a performance for the ages, an effort that has never been matched and is unlikely to ever find a peer. The American men won all but one event and shredded the record books in a team showing that was legendary.

10. BRIGITHA BREAKS BARRIER

In 1976, Dutchwoman Enith Brigitha made history when she became the first black swimmer to medal at the Olympic Games, earning bronze medals in the 100 and

200 freestyle. Like many others, though, Brigitha was a victim of East Germany's systematic doping program, which robbed her of greater Olympic glory.

11. POLITICAL PAWNS

The powerhouse American program was missing from the 1980 Games in Moscow, due to the boycott instituted by President Jimmy Carter in response to the Soviet Union's invasion of Afghanistan. The decision denied many athletes the opportunity to chase their Olympic dreams.

12. ROWDY'S REACTION

At the height of his career, Rowdy Gaines was denied the opportunity to find Olympic glory, with the U.S. boycott of the 1980 Games in Moscow keeping him at home. But 4 years later, Gaines atoned for his missed chance, with some critical coaching advice playing a major role in his success.

13. A TIE GAME

At the 1984 Olympics, American teammates Carrie Steinseifer and Nancy Hogshead touched the wall, looked to the scoreboard, and smiled at each other. They had tied for the gold medal in the 100 freestyle, marking the first shared gold medal in the sport's Olympic history.

14. THE BEST OF BIONDI

Before Michael Phelps's name became synonymous with Mark Spitz, it was Matt Biondi who was measured against Spitz and what he achieved at the 1972 Olympic Games. At the 1988 Games in Seoul, Biondi did not match Spitz's seven–gold medal performance, but he won seven medals overall, including five gold, and left a legacy as one of the greatest performers in the sport's history.

15. NESTY NETS GOLD

When Suriname's Anthony Nesty got his hands on the wall a hundredth of a second ahead of American Matt Biondi in the 100 butterfly at the 1988 Games in Seoul, it marked the first time that a black swimmer won a gold medal at the Olympic Games.

16. THE DRAGON SLAYER

Ranked 46th in the world in the 200 freestyle entering the 1988 Olympic Games in Seoul, Australia's Duncan Armstrong was an afterthought in medal discussions. When the championship final was over, however, Armstrong was the gold medalist, and his stunning triumph set off one of the greatest coaching celebrations the sport has seen.

17. A TALE OF REDEMPTION

After failing to qualify for the 1988 Games in Seoul as the heavy favorite in the 100 butterfly, Pablo Morales retired and began the pursuit of a law degree. However, the urge to compete again grabbed Morales ahead of the 1992 Games, which turned into a fairy tale when Morales claimed the gold medal in his prime event.

18. GOLD MEDAL GUITAR

Before the 2000 Olympic Games in Sydney, the United States had never lost the 400 freestyle relay in Olympic competition, thus allowing Gary Hall Jr. to claim that the Americans would smash the upstart Australians like guitars. After the race, however, the Aussies were strumming along to their national anthem.

19. ERIC THE EEL

At the 2000 Olympic Games in Sydney, a swimmer far from medal contention briefly captured the fancy of the sport and the thousands of fans who filled the Sydney Aquatic Centre. The world's media gave him a clever nickname, and he has gone down in swimming lore, his story a feel-good tale.

20. A TIE BETWEEN TEAMMATES

Training together at the Phoenix Swim Club and living as roommates in the Olympic Village, veteran Gary Hall Jr. and upstart Anthony Ervin wrote an intriguing chapter in the history of sprinting when they shared the gold medal in the 50 freestyle at the 2000 Olympics in Sydney.

21. RACE OF THE CENTURY

The 200 freestyle had enough substance at the 2004 Olympics, thanks to a repeat clash between the Netherlands' Pieter van den Hoogenband and Australia's Ian Thorpe. But when Michael Phelps entered the fray, the race became something special and one of the most anticipated events in Olympic history.

22. AN ILLEGAL KICKSTART

The final of the 100 breaststroke at the 2004 Olympics in Athens was shrouded in controversy after Japan's Kosuke Kitajima was shown performing an illegal kick on the way to defeating American Brendan Hansen. The move by Kitajima set off a charge of cheating by Hansen's teammate and close friend Aaron Peirsol and proved to be the impetus for a rule change in the stroke.

23. AN ANCHOR'S WAY

When Jason Lezak entered the water for the United States on the anchor leg of the 400 freestyle relay at the 2008 Olympic Games in Beijing, the race was seemingly over. Lezak trailed Frenchman Alain Bernard by a body length, and overcoming that deficit appeared impossible. But Lezak, behind the greatest anchor leg in history, gradually reeled in Bernard to give the United States an improbable gold medal.

24. A HALF-STROKE FOR HISTORY

With just a few strokes remaining in the 100-meter butterfly duel between Michael Phelps and Milorad Cavic at the 2008 Olympic Games in Beijing, Phelps's pursuit of eight gold medals looked over. Cavic had a visible lead, until Phelps dipped into his bag of magic tricks and pulled out an improbable victory.

25. AGE IS JUST A NUMBER

Despite missing out on the gold medal by a hundredth of a second in the 50-meter freestyle at the 2008 Games in Beijing, Dara Torres defied age—and became an icon for middle-aged women—by winning three silver medals at the tender age of 41.

Acknowledgments

Others will argue, but there is no doubt in my mind that I am the luckiest man in the world—blessed with a wonderful family, immediate and extended, and the most loyal friends. Not a day goes by in which I do not stop and shake my head at the good fortune of my life.

As these projects arise and deadlines near, it is always comforting to have a support system at home, which makes the process possible. My wife, Dana, has been amazing. Whether providing a few words of encouragement or simply giving me the time to work, she is a godsend. Each day is better than the last, filled with many laughs, smiles, and memories.

Our twin daughters, Taylor and Tiernan, bring excitement from sunrise to sunset, and there is no doubt that their on-the-way baby sister will follow suit upon her arrival into our lives. They also deserve credit for some of the work in this book, for I cannot count the times that they have wandered over when Dad was working and pounded the keyboard until they were satisfied with their contribution.

I cannot thank my mom and dad enough for the guidance that they have provided through the years. From an early age, they taught me to chase my dreams and to battle through the tough times. My mom has always been the emotional glue of our family, while my dad instilled the traits of hard work, determination, and loyalty. I will never be able to repay them for what they have provided.

Finally, a big thank-you goes to Tom Robinson, a man whom I have been able to call a friend for more than a decade. Tom took the time to educate me about the sport of swimming. As the longtime coach of Radnor High School's highly successful swim program, Tom did not have to teach a clueless kid—but he did—and his kindness and patience are appreciated more than words can say. The best part of meeting Tom—who graciously took time to read the chapters of this book as they were written—is that he has become a good friend.

From family to friends, there is only one way to look at my life: *Damn lucky!*

Introduction

It has become commonplace for die-hard, casual, and nonsports fans to get caught up every 4 years in that global event known as the Olympic Games. Actually, it used to be every 4 years when the Olympic phenomenon took over, but when the International Olympic Committee decided to alternate the Summer and Winter Games on a 2-year basis starting in 1994, it became even more frequent for televisions to be tuned to the various sports.

Whether individuals hail from the United States, France, Australia, or some other nation, there is something intriguing and captivating about watching an Olympic event unfold. Oftentimes, fans get caught up in national pride, rooting for their countrymen and countrywomen to prevail, so their flag will rise to the rafters as the national anthem is played. A degree of appreciation also factors into the equation, with fans cheering on athletes out of respect for the hours of hard work required to simply advance to the Olympic stage.

My first memory of the Olympic Games is from 1984, specifically Carl Lewis running the final of the 100-meter dash in Los Angeles. Because I was a 7-year-old at the time, I am not going to pretend that I recall many details of the race, but I certainly remember Lewis's image on the television screen. Since my dad was a football, basketball, and track-and-field coach, it was normal for the television to be tuned into some sort of athletic event—no wonder why I grew up a sports junkie and have spent part of my professional career in the sports journalism business.

When Scarecrow Press approached me about serving as editor of its swimming series, the first two titles were fairly obvious. One needed to take a look at the best athletes to ever dive into a pool—thus, the creation of *They Ruled the Pool: The 100 Greatest Swimmers in History*. The second title, due to the sport's individual nature, needed to examine the fiercest rivalries. As a result, Matthew De George produced *Duels in the Pool: Swimming's Greatest Rivalries*.

It soon became time to expand the series, at which point another fact became obvious. Because swimming is one of the highest-profile sports on the Olympic schedule—particularly with the popularity ushered in by Michael Phelps—a book featuring the top Olympic moments was a no-brainer. So, here we are with *The Most Memorable Moments in Olympic Swimming*.

To say that there were plenty of moments from which to choose would be a massive understatement, what with swimming part of the Olympic schedule since the first edition of the Modern Games in Athens in 1896. The dilemma would be selecting the moments for inclusion and how to sift through the possibilities in a manner that produced the best. Of course, some were obvious, and others required measured debate. Meanwhile, the research conducted revealed several moments that did not immediately jump to mind but certainly warranted entry.

Top-10 and top-25 lists are the most common when tackling a project such as this, and with the rich history of Olympic swimming, picking 25 moments was the way to go. Here is how we arrived at the 25 that line the pages of this book.

GETTING STARTED

A calming aspect of this project from the start was the fact that once the 25 greatest moments were selected, there would be no intent to rank them. To simply make the cut verified the excellence of the chosen moments, and there did not seem to be a need to further rate them. Additionally, comparing the various moments would be impossible in terms of establishing a level field of judgment.

While some of the moments were selected on the basis of their context in swimming history, such as Mark Spitz winning seven gold medals at the 1972 Olympics in Munich, other moments were based on their emotional meaning, such as Pablo Morales winning gold at the 1992 Games, just a few months after his mother's death and 4 years after he stunningly failed to qualify for the 1988 Games. How could physical excellence, such as what Spitz delivered, possibly be gauged against emotional impact, such as Morales's story? The short answer: they couldn't. And that is how the decision to organize the moments chronologically came to be.

After deciding against a 1-to-25 ranking, the next step in the process was simple: pick the moments. Getting to that point required a considerable amount of reading, research, and discussion with experts in the sport, including fellow journalists, longtime coaches, and hardcore fans who have a thorough understanding of what has taken place in each Olympiad.

The first step in selecting the moments necessitated looking at each Olympiad on an individual basis, in search of key accomplishments and storylines that stood out. Once this audit was conducted, the 100 or so moments that were recorded had to be pared down to a workable list. It was actually a fairly easy task, as some of the moments that were noted during the first run-through clearly did not carry the clout to make the final list.

After the weeding process, there were about 50 moments for consideration, which meant that half of those entries had to go. How did that cut unfold? Well, it wasn't easy, but it was manageable. It was a matter of looking at the moments and weighing their prominence.

THE MEASUREMENT OF IMPACT

In selecting the moments for the top 25 and the 10 that just missed out, it was important that all held some sort of significance. But "significance" had a variety of definitions in this endeavor:

- Some moments were considered history-making achievements, performances that had never been seen before or were so dominant that they stood on their own pedestal. Included in this category were such accomplishments as Mark Spitz's seven-gold showing in Munich; Dawn Fraser's threepeat in the 100 freestyle at the 1956, 1960, and 1964 Olympics; and the effort of the 1976 U.S. men's Olympic team, which won all but one event in Montreal.
- Some moments featured an emotional impact, a sentimental touch that complemented the achievement. In this category is where we found stories such as that of Duncan Armstrong, whose 1988 victory in the 200 freestyle featured the toppling of several world-record holders and touched off a celebration for the ages by his coach, Laurie Lawrence. Here, too, fell the story of Eric Moussambani, the swimmer from Equatorial Guinea who barely completed the 100 freestyle at the 2000 Games in Sydney but whose effort and battle to the finish were inspiring.
- There were also moments that were thrilling, those performances that stopped the heart due to their down-to-the-wire nature. Included in this category were the only two ties in Olympic swimming history; the 1972 duel between Sweden's Gunnar Larsson and American Tim McKee, which was decided by two thousandths of a second; and Jason Lezak's remarkable anchor leg, which carried the United States to gold in the 400 freestyle relay at the 2008 Olympics and preserved Michael Phelps's pursuit of an Olympic-record eight gold medals.
- And, there were moments which transcended the sport. While swimming put the moments on the map, there was much more to the story than what took place in the water. In this category fell the systematic doping program put into effect by East Germany and the decision by United States president Jimmy Carter to boycott the 1980 Olympics in Moscow, thus denying hundreds of athletes their Olympic dreams.

AT WHAT TIME?

A glance through the moments picked for inclusion in this book reveals that the majority of the selections are from the latter half of the 20th century into the 21st century. While a few instances of selections are from the early 20th century, notably Johnny Weissmuller, coverage from the 1920s (give or take a decade) did not lend itself to an archival sense. More, the fact that the sport was headlined by just a handful of countries limited the number of enthralling storylines.

But as time passed and with the enhancement of television, print, and Internet coverage of sporting events—particularly, the Olympic Games—documentation of the greatest moments became an easier task. Athletes' stories received broader press, and their tales became familiar with those connected to the Olympic movement. Simply, they grew in depth, especially the stories that went beyond the angle of "Who finished first?"

Among the most influential individuals in the expansion of the Olympic reach was Bud Greenspan, the famed documentarian whose death in 2010 left a void in Olympic coverage in general and Olympic storytelling in particular. No one has come close to matching the completeness of Greenspan's coverage.

Olympiad after Olympiad, Greenspan sought out the best stories of the era and unveiled them in eloquent fashion, the sporting aspect of the story perfectly mixed with the human interest element. Because of work like this, more recent moments in Olympic lore have received greater publicity. It should not be surprising that Greenspan's work paved the way for the inclusion of several Olympic moments in this book, such as Rowdy Gaines's gold medal triumph in the 100 freestyle at the 1984 Olympics or the stunning upset registered by Australian Duncan Armstrong in the 200 freestyle at the 1988 Games in Seoul.

Although newer stories account for the greater percentage of chapters, long-ago days were not ignored. It was a simple decision to include Weissmuller, among the first stars in the sport and a multitime Olympic champion before the silver screen became his milieu. It was only logical to include the debut of women in Olympic competition. And it was an easy call to feature Dawn Fraser, the first individual to win the same event at three consecutive Olympiads.

On the whole, however, there was no intent to select a specific number of moments from each decade. Rather, the story—and its depth—dictated which moments made the cut and which did not. There is confidence that the 25 tales that "made the team" are the best.

THE RESULT

One of the beautiful parts of sports is how it generates debate and fosters healthy discussion among historians and fans. In no way is the list included in this book a be-all, end-all collection. When individuals look at the 25 moments within this work, there is no doubt someone will say, "I would have included this moment over that one." Truthfully, I hope that type of analysis takes place. It's healthy and part of the fabric of sports fandom.

But whether the readership agrees or disagrees with the Olympic moments high-lighted, this much is inarguable: The moments that are included are all worthy of inclusion, and the thought and research that went into this project were exhaustive. The book was a joy to write, just as it is a joy to watch the wonder that is the Olympics.

1

Welcome the Women

Sixteen years after the men started racing at the Olympic Games, women's events were added to the schedule at the 1912 Games in Stockholm, albeit in limited fashion. Australian Fanny Durack became the first female champion, winning the 100 freestyle.

Not long after Hungarian Alfred Hajos became the first Olympic swimming champion—winning the gold medal in the 100 freestyle at the 1896 Games in Athens—Australia's Sarah "Fanny" Durack developed the urge to learn to swim. It wasn't that Durack, a youngster at the time, was inspired by Hajos's efforts or the performances by any other male swimmer.

Rather, Durack's desire to swim was triggered out of necessity and in the pursuit of peace of mind. While on vacation as a 9-year-old, Durack struggled with the surf in her native land, and it was that experience that convinced her to become water safe. It was also a decision that made Durack swimming's first female superstar.

From 1896, when the first Modern Games were held in the birthplace of the Ancient Olympics, through 1908, only men were allowed to compete in swimming at the Olympics. During that time, the likes of Hajos, American Charles Daniels, Great Britain's Henry Taylor, and Hungary's Zoltan Halmay emerged as the sport's standouts.

It was not as if women were banned from the Olympics altogether during that stretch of time, as female athletes competed in events such as sailing, tennis, and equestrian as early as the 1900 Games in Paris. Swimming, though, did not create a coed program until the 1912 Games, which were held in Stockholm, Sweden.

When it was announced that women would be invited to compete in Stockholm, some countries jumped at the opportunity, while others were disinterested. Only 27 women took part in the two swimming events—the 100 freestyle and the 400 freestyle relay—with host Sweden and Great Britain sending six athletes each. Australia sent two swimmers, Durack and Mina Wylie, while the United States opted to send no women, despite fielding a team of seven men.

While Durack had put together an impressive career, Wylie actually held the upper hand over her countrywoman in the lead-up to the 1912 Games. Wylie beat Durack on several occasions at the Australian Championships and was considered a gold medal favorite as much as Durack, who had the higher public profile.

Getting to the Olympics, however, proved to be an issue for Durack and Wylie, with politics playing a role. Considering the role that politics has played throughout the history of the Olympic Games, maybe it was fitting that Durack and Wylie had to play a waiting game.

"The Aussie men in charge of selecting the team for the 1912 Games declared that it was a waste of time and money to send women to Sweden," wrote Craig Lord of the website SwimVortex.

> The rule book didn't help, either. The New South Wales Ladies' Amateur Swimming Association regulations held that no women could compete at events where men were present. A public outcry resulted in a vote and rule change at the association and Durack and Wylie were allowed to make the journey to Europe—provided they paid for themselves. The wife of Hugh McIntosh, a sporting and theatrical entrepreneur and newspaper proprietor, launched a successful appeal for funds and with money donated by the public, family and friends, Durack sailed for Sweden via London, where she was reported to have trained half a mile a day.

The competition pool was hardly high-tech, constructed in Stockholm Harbor and consisting of salt water. But Durack wasn't derailed by the conditions. Representing Australasia—a combined team from Australia and New Zealand—Durack opened her Olympic career in grand fashion, setting a world record of 1:19.8 during the qualifying heats of the 100 freestyle. She followed by easily winning her semifinal, then capturing the gold medal with a time of 1:22.2, more than 3 seconds quicker than Wylie.

Great Britain's Daisy Curwen was expected to be a medal contender in the final, but the former world-record holder was forced to withdraw from the competition after the semifinal round due to a bout of appendicitis. It was Curwen's world record that Durack broke during the qualifying heats.

With Durack and Wylie the only Aussies competing in swimming, Australasia could not field a squad for the 400 freestyle relay, although it tried. Durack and Wylie offered to swim two legs each if Australasia was given the chance to race, but officials denied the request, and Great Britain's quartet of Belle Moore, Jennie Fletcher, Annie Speirs, and Irene Steer went on to win the gold medal by nearly 12 seconds over Germany. Fletcher was the bronze medalist behind Durack and Wylie in the 100 freestyle and spoke of the limited practice time that she and her teammates had in preparation for the 1912 Games.

"We swam only after working hours, and they were 12 hours and six days a week," Fletcher said. "We were told bathing suits were shocking and indecent, and even when entering competition, we were covered with a floor-length cloak until we entered the water."

With only two women's events, as opposed to the seven on the men's program, there is no telling what else Durack could have done if given the chance to contest additional events. But a lack of equality in the Olympic schedule has been more commonplace than not during the 100-plus years of the Games. From the first time that women competed in swimming at the Olympics through the 1972 Games in Munich, men's events always outnumbered women's events.

And while men and women each competed in 13 events at the 1976 and 1980 Games, there were fewer women's events over the next three Olympiads. Since 1996, however, the number of events between the sexes has matched, albeit with a caveat. Through the 2012 Olympics in London, there was inequality in the length of the longest events on each program. While men's distance swimmers contested the 1500 freestyle as their sex's longest event, women covered just more than half that distance via the 800 freestyle. There is talk, however, about the programs matching by the 2016 Games in Rio de Janeiro.

A parallel can be found in the history of track and field. It wasn't until the 1984 Games in Los Angeles in which women contested the marathon, and in years prior, women's distances were capped at 1,500 meters, while male athletes were given the opportunity to double in the 5,000 and 10,000.

From 1912 to 1918, Durack set 11 world records over various distances, including 3 in the 100-meter freestyle. Her fastest time of 1:16.2 from 1915 lasted for 5 years, until American Ethelda Bleibtrey won Olympic gold in 1:14.4. A Durack-Bleibtrey duel would have been a highlight event of the 1920 Games, but illness prevented Durack from racing.

After being denied the chance to defend her Olympic title in 1916 due to the cancellation of the Games by World War I, Durack was hoping to repeat in 1920, but appendicitis put an end to that dream. More, Durack came down with typhoid fever and pneumonia a week before Australia's athletes were scheduled to sail to Europe for the Antwerp Games.

In between competitions, Durack took part in numerous world tours with Wylie, in which they would race each other and demonstrate the Australian crawl, the stroke that Durack made famous and used to become a world-record holder. Durack's vast achievements earned her induction into the International Swimming Hall of Fame in 1967, the third year of the hall's existence.

"Fanny Durack not only took on all comers the world over, but beat all comers the world over for eight years in the formative years of women's swimming," reads Durack's profile in the International Swimming Hall of Fame.

4

Chapter 1

CHART NO. 1.1

Here is a look at the number of events for men and women at each Olympic Games. It wasn't until 1976 that male and female athletes were offered the same number of events, and that equality only lasted two Olympiads. Since 1996, men and women have each contested 16 events.

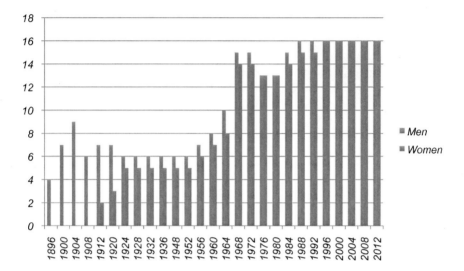

2

Before He Swung from Vines

To most people, Johnny Weissmuller was Tarzan and a star of motion pictures. Before he rose to fame for his historic yell, though, Weissmuller established himself as a legendary swimmer, winning back-to-back Olympic gold medals in the 100 freestyle at the 1924 and 1928 Games.

Most recollections of Johnny Weissmuller paint a man running around bare-chested and wearing nothing more than a loin cloth. A cinematic star during the first half of the 20th century, Weissmuller was the human King of the Jungle, perfecting the Tarzan scream while becoming the most famed actor to handle the role on the big screen.

Yet, before he went Hollywood and earned a star on the Walk of Fame, Weissmuller etched his name in the annals of swimming, becoming the biggest star of his time and an Olympic champion. Even today, nearly a century after Weissmuller rode his freestyle stroke to multiple gold medals and numerous world-record performances, he is revered as one of the greatest performers in the history of the sport.

Ask anyone with a vast knowledge of swimming about the greatest Americans to ever hit the pool, and you will likely get a six-name list spanning 100 years. One will say Duke Kahanamoku and Weissmuller were the stars of the early years, setting the table for Don Schollander and Mark Spitz and, eventually, Matt Biondi and Michael Phelps.

How Weissmuller came to stardom is a unique story. Like most swimmers, he was in the water at a young age, instructed by a doctor to start building muscle after dealing with a bout of polio. Yet, while Weissmuller was a member of a YMCA team in Chicago, the extent of his talent was not immediately realized.

Coached by William Bachrach, Weissmuller was kept out of the public eye by his mentor until the finer details of the sport were enhanced. It wasn't until Bachrach was satisfied with Weissmuller's skill and all-around ability that he allowed him to reveal it to a wider audience.

"Bachrach kept young Weissmuller under wraps for a year, refining his start and stroke," a *Chicago Tribune* article stated. "In August 1921, he turned his protégé loose to win national championships in the 50–yard and 220–yard distances. He never lost a swimming competition after that."

The unchaining of Weissmuller set in motion what proved to be the most illustrious career of any swimmer at the time, as Weissmuller went on to set more than 50 world records and win more than 50 national championships. More impressive, his excellence spanned a number of distances and not just the freestyle stroke.

Rather than focus on the shortest distances contested at the time, Weissmuller set world records—at one point or another—in the 100, 200, 400, and 800 distances. For good measure, he was also a stellar backstroker, even setting a world record in the stroke. Further setting Weissmuller apart was the fact that he was so far ahead of his time.

The future film star did not just establish world records; his global standards lasted for years, most notably his marks in the 100 and 200 freestyles. In the 100 free, Weissmuller was the first man to break the 1-minute barrier, and he held the world record from 1922 to 1934. In the 200 free, he stood as the world-record holder from 1922 to 1935, shaving 11 seconds off the world record between the first and last time that he set the record.

It was in Olympic competition, however, where Weissmuller excelled the greatest and forever made himself a household name. To attain that Olympic glory, Weissmuller first had to pull off one of the great bits of deception in sports.

As the 1924 Olympics in Paris neared, questions surrounding Weissmuller's American citizenship began to surface and with good reason. Weissmuller was actually born—according to official records—on June 2, 1904, in the small town of Friedorf, part of Romania. Although he moved to the United States with his parents 7 months later, he was not an American citizen.

This fact became an issue leading up to the Paris Games because Weissmuller needed official documentation of his citizenship to secure an American passport, which would enable his travel to the Olympics. For this reason, Weissmuller put into motion a major ruse, one that proved to be successful.

His father once insisted that Weissmuller was born in Chicago, but this was later changed to Windber, a small town in Pennsylvania. Indeed, a Weissmuller was born in this town, but it was Johnny's younger brother Peter. Using this familial connection to his advantage, Weissmuller got hold of baptismal records from St. John Cantius Catholic Church for his brother Petrus Weissmuller. Inserted between the first and last names and in different ink and penmanship was "John." Weissmuller asserted that this official record was his, and it met the needs to allow his participation in the 1924 Olympics.

"After satisfying Olympic and government officials of his American citizenship, Weissmuller joined the U.S. team and swam in Paris," stated a 1984 *Sports Illustrated* article on the doubts concerning Weissmuller's citizenship. "He became an instant national hero. It seemed nobody now wanted to raise questions about his citizenship.

Claiming Windber as his birthplace not only gave Weissmuller the opportunity to produce 'proof' of his American birth but also provided him with a new hometown, which in later years would welcome him back as its most famous native son."

Weissmuller ran with the deceit for years ahead, even celebrating a day in his honor in Windber in 1950, years after his Olympic exploits. On that day, Weissmuller went as far as to say, "I have always wanted a hometown, and now I have one. This is the biggest thrill I ever had in my life and this includes the events when I won the Olympic titles in 1924 and 1928 and was presented medals by the queen of the Netherlands."

Throughout his life, Weissmuller ensured that his secret was well protected. He never told his family of his true birthplace, including his five wives and only son, Johnny Jr., and he told his biographer that he was born in Windber, Pennsylvania. According to the *Sports Illustrated* article, those in Romania who knew the true story of his birth in their homeland did not want to ruin his success, for they were proud of what he achieved.

After Weissmuller died in 1984, his son learned of the truth when interviewed about the topic. After the initial shock, he toasted his father to Arlene Mueller of *Sports Illustrated*, "To the old man. He sure could keep a secret."

If there were ever concerns about Weissmuller's accomplishments being stricken due to his trickery, it seems that those days have passed. Instead, Weissmuller is revered for his excellence in the pool. With his citizenship issues resolved, Weissmuller went to the 1924 Olympics and won three gold medals. He won individual titles in the 100 and 400 freestyles and helped the 800 freestyle relay to victory. For good measure, he added a bronze medal as a member of the American water polo team.

Weissmuller's triumph in the 100 freestyle was the marquee win, as he prevailed by more than 2 seconds over Kahanamoku, the Olympic champion in the event in 1912 and 1920 and a likely three-time Olympic champion, had it not been for the cancellation of the 1916 Games due to World War I. While Weissmuller had already started setting world records, his win over Kahanamoku marked the official changing of the guard.

As for the 400 freestyle, it served as an exhibition of Weissmuller's range. With the 200 freestyle not on the Olympic program, Weissmuller was forced to take on a middle-distance event for his second discipline. While Weissmuller was the world-record holder and the first man under 5 minutes in the event, he was not a lock to succeed against such opposition as Arne Borg of Sweden and Andrew "Boy" Charlton of Australia.

Borg and Charlton were better suited to the 400 freestyle and therefore had the ability to take Weissmuller down. But Weissmuller reached into his deep talent and bettered Borg by a little more than a second, an impressive feat considering that Borg became the world-record holder just a few months after the Olympic Games.

The winning ways continued for Weissmuller through the 1928 Olympics in Amsterdam, where Weissmuller repeated as champion of the 100 freestyle and again led the United States to gold in the 800 freestyle relay. When his amateur career came to a close, Weissmuller had never lost a race.

The dominance exhibited by Weissmuller in Paris and Amsterdam was nothing short of phenomenal. He clearly showed himself to be in another realm than the competition, leaving his foes to compete for the minor medals. It was no surprise when he was inducted into the International Swimming Hall of Fame in 1965.

Still swimming and working for a bathing suit company 2 years after the Amsterdam Games, Weissmuller was approached about taking a screen test while in Los Angeles for the upcoming movie *Tarzan the Ape Man*. He went to MGM Studios for the shoot, along with 150 other men, but never thought that the test would pan out.

"I had to climb a tree and then run past the camera carrying a girl," he said.

There were 150 actors trying for the part, so after lunch, I took off for Oregon on my next stop for the swim suit outfit. Somebody called me on the phone and said "Johnny, you got it." "Got what?" "You're Tarzan." "What happened to those other 150 guys?" "They picked you."

So the producer asked me my name and he said it would never go. "We'll have to shorten it," he said. "Weissmuller is too long. It will never go on a marquee." The director butted in. "Don't you ever read the papers? This guy is the world's greatest swimmer." The producer said he only read the trade papers, but okay, I could keep my name and he told the writers, "put a lot of swimming in the movie, because this guy can swim."

"So you see why I owe everything to swimming," Weissmuller said. "It not only made my name, it saved my name. Without swimming, I'd be a nobody. Who ever heard of Jon Weis, marquee or no marquee."

Weissmuller starred in 12 Tarzan films and enjoyed other roles in movies and television. He was a high-paid star and affirmed himself as that unique person who could close one career and excel at an equally successful level in another.

Still, it was swimming—namely, what he achieved in the Olympic Games—that made his vast success a possibility.

3

The Dawn of Greatness

At the 1964 Olympics in Tokyo, Australian Dawn Fraser made history by becoming the first swimmer—male or female—to win an event at three consecutive Olympiads, accomplishing the feat in the 100 freestyle. In the half century that has passed since that achievement, only two other individuals have joined Fraser in that exclusive club.

Ask several experts on the sport for their opinion on the greatest female swimmer of all time, and four answers might emerge. Arguments can be made for Americans Tracy Caulkins and Janet Evans, along with Hungarian Krisztina Egerszegi. Also a candidate for top-woman status is Australian Dawn Fraser, a freestyle sensation whose marker in history will never be moved.

At the time of the 1956 Olympics, Australia was in need of an aquatic spark. The country was an also-ran on the international stage, an unacceptable standing, and it was Fraser who played a leading role in lifting the Land of Oz. By the time that her career came to a close at the 1964 Olympics in Tokyo, the legacy of Australian swimming had been restored, and Fraser was a goddess of the water.

The launch of Fraser's legend started in 1950 when she first crossed paths with Harry Gallagher, the man who became her coach and molded her career into something special. They built a relationship based equally on respect and occasional clashes, which brought out the best in Fraser. If Fraser did not want to do something, she let Gallagher know. If Gallagher needed something done, he found a way. As time went on and both aged and understood the other better, their relationship blossomed further.

"Dawn was a horror. She told me I was a deadbeat, to drop dead, to piss off, to get lost," Gallagher said.

> She wasn't going to do what I wanted her to do. No guy would ever get her to do what she didn't want to do. She had wild aggression. She reminded me of a wild mare in the hills that you had put the lightest lead on to keep her under control. She wanted to do

her own thing. If you had to guide her, it had to be very subtly, so she didn't understand that she was being manipulated. I used to say that, you know, "Dawn, no girl has ever done this before, and I don't think you can do it either, but you just might be able to do it." She'd say, "What do you bloody well mean? Of course I can bloody well do it."

Over time, the athlete-coach bond between Fraser and Gallagher turned into something magical. The world records started to drop in 1956, the same time that Fraser started to eclipse Lorraine Crapp, formerly coached by Gallagher, as the premier Australian swimmer. And when the success started, it did not cease until Fraser tied the bow on her career.

"I probably have a different mental approach to swimming than most people," Fraser said.

I actually enjoy training most of the time. When I don't want to train, I don't. If it comes, it comes, and I don't force myself. Nine years ago, when I started swimming seriously, I did absolutely everything my coach, Harry Gallagher, told me to, but then two years ago I began using my own judgment more and more, and we both feel that this arrangement is better. In other words, our relationship is not that of coach and pupil, but more like that of brother and sister.

Although she was a major talent in the 200 freestyle and could stretch up to the 400 freestyle to be a factor on the international scene, Fraser made her name in the 100 freestyle, considered the sport's blue-ribbon discipline. In what was a changing of the guard, Fraser won her first Olympic title in the event in 1956, setting a world record while turning back a challenge from Crapp.

The records continued to fall to Fraser in the interim between those 1956 Games in Melbourne and the 1960 Olympics in Rome, where Fraser repeated as champion of the 100 freestyle. But it is what unfolded 4 years later, in Fraser's third Olympiad, that stamped her legendary status.

With Gallagher providing guidance and motivation, Fraser prepared for the 1964 Olympics in Tokyo by continuing to lower her world records and becoming the first woman to break the 1-minute barrier in the 100 freestyle. Despite battling injury and heartache, Fraser followed her previous Olympic triumphs with another victory, becoming the first person to win a swimming event in three straight Olympiads. The honor made Fraser as acclaimed an Olympian as existed and left many to wonder whether her feat would be matched again. Getting to that moment, however, was not easy—on various levels.

If Fraser's feat of three consecutive Olympic gold medals in the same event was appreciated in 1964, history provides greater context. In the half century since Fraser produced her trifecta, only two other individuals have matched Fraser's accomplishment—Hungarian Krisztina Egerszegi and Olympic legend Michael Phelps.

Egerszegi, considered among the top-five female swimmers of all time, won the 200 backstroke at the 1988 Olympics, 1992 Games, and 1996 Olympics. Never threatened in any of her triumphs, Egerszegi saw her margin of victory grow in each of her Olympiads, and her name is often associated with that of Fraser's due to their shared historic achievements.

Because Phelps achieved everything that there is to accomplish in the sport, it is only fitting that he shares special air with Fraser and Egerszegi. In the 200 individual medley and 100 butterfly, Phelps was the Olympic champion in 2004, 2008, and 2012—those combined six victories accounting for a portion of the 18 gold medals that he accrued during his sensational career.

Although Fraser raced over three Olympiads, her longevity was a deviation from the norm during her era. Nowadays, it is much more common for athletes to remain active in the sport for longer durations, a fact that makes the exclusivity of Fraser and company even more impressive. Surely, additional members will join the club in the years ahead, but Fraser will always hold the status of president emeritus.

Having won gold medals in the 100 freestyle at the 1956 and 1960 Games, Fraser felt considerable pressure as the Tokyo Games neared. Yet, that pressure was far from the biggest obstacle that she faced. Rather, Fraser had to overcome physical and emotional injuries suffered in an automobile accident that claimed the life of her mother and injured Fraser's sister and a close friend. Fraser was the driver of the car.

During the early hours of March 9, 1964, 7 months before the Olympics in To-kyo, Fraser offered to give her sister a ride home following a fund-raising event, with her mother and friend riding in the backseat of the vehicle. As Fraser was driving, she suddenly came upon a truck and had to veer out of the way, causing the car to flip over. "I had this car, which was the first car I'd ever driven that had power steering," Fraser recalled in her autobiography, *What I Learned along the Way*. "As I pulled the car to swerve it, I rolled the car."

Fraser's mother was pronounced dead on arrival at the hospital, with Fraser and the other two passengers suffering injuries. When Fraser awoke at the hospital, she was not immediately informed of her mother's fate. Eventually, her brother informed Fraser of their mother's death, but he told his sister that their mother died of a heart attack, not from injuries sustained in the crash.

As Fraser prepared to write her autobiography, she learned the true story of her mother's death, a fact that was difficult to accept. However, Fraser found some solace in having her doubts about the incident answered. "I was led to believe by my family for many, many years, up until three years ago, that my mother had died prior to the accident," Fraser wrote in her tell-all book. "I did not feel good inside, but I know I've wiped away that question mark in my mind. Over the years, I've realized you can beat yourself up at night, lose sleep . . . but you can't change the past. My parents taught me to accept things the way they were, the rights and the wrongs . . . and to learn from my mistakes."

Following the crash, Fraser not only had to deal with the emotional toll of losing her mother but also had to battle through the injuries that she endured, including a chipped vertebra. Fraser spent 9 weeks with her neck and spine in a brace, and doctors advised her against diving into a pool, due to the added trauma that it could cause. It wasn't until she raced in Tokyo, with a third Olympic crown in the 100 freestyle on the line, that she dove off the starting blocks with full force.

Given the injuries that she suffered—physically and mentally—few would have blamed Fraser had she abandoned pursuit of another Olympic title. But Fraser was determined to forge ahead and chase history, even if the risk of failure dangled in front of her. Never one to back away from a challenge, Fraser attacked the Tokyo Games with the same fervor as an athlete chasing her first Olympic gold medal.

"I put myself under a lot of pressure by deciding to go to Tokyo and I also put myself under a lot of pressure to compete in the same event in three Olympics," Fraser said. "I had, at the back of mind, that this was for my mother because we were saving up for my mother to go to Tokyo with me [before the accident]. I just imagined that she was there and that I was doing it for her."

Although Fraser was the world-record holder in the 100 freestyle and the two-time defending champion, there were reasonable questions concerning her ability to prevail again. Naturally, there were questions surrounding her health and fitness while coming off the car accident. Additionally, the United States boasted a teen upstart in Sharon Stouder, a youngster expected to give Fraser all that she could handle.

Relying on her experience, vast talent, and deep passion to win for her mother and make history, Fraser covered her two laps in an Olympic-record time of 59.5, with Stouder earning the silver medal in 59.9. The bronze medal went to the United States' Kathy Ellis in 1:00.8. The effort was revered in sporting circles.

"She was up against it," said Harry Gordon, Australia's official Olympic historian.

> Her whole story is one of triumph over adversity. That was another stunning example of it. I think that was the toughest test of her career. She just didn't want to be beaten, which is what you find about most of the really good athletes. Her own individual makeup was such that if she competed, there was no way she wasn't going to win. It's only when you look back and see the achievement that Dawn made you realize how phenomenal it was.

As talented as Fraser was in the pool, she was equally known for her opposition of authority and penchant for finding trouble—and trouble is exactly what Fraser found after she completed her gold-medal triple. With a pass to leave the Athletes' Village and stay at the Imperial Palace Hotel while filming a commercial, Fraser met up with an Australian team doctor, Howard Toyne, and Des Piper, a member of the bronze medal–winning field hockey team. Together, the trio planned on obtaining a few souvenir Olympic flags, found lining the street leading to the Imperial Palace, the main residence of the emperor of Japan.

Fraser and her mates managed to get two flags down but not without alerting police. The threesome tried to run away, but Fraser fell and had to sit on a park bench. After Toyne and Piper were caught, police found a flag on Fraser, arrested her, and took her to the police station. After the police found out that it was Fraser—an athlete of considerable standing—they decided to let the Australians go. The next day, the lieutenant at the police station gave Fraser the flag to keep.

"After showing them my gold medal and my dog tags, you know, [the police] were still very disgusted that I'd . . . that it was me, but they couldn't believe that I would do that," Fraser said. "And then he explained to me that it was a stealing offense, it could mean a jail term. And they decided then because of who I was, Dawn Fraser, they let us off."

The flag incident was the third strike for Fraser as far as Australian Swimming was concerned. Earlier in the Olympiad, Fraser angered officials by marching in the Opening Ceremony, against orders to skip the event and prepare for competition. Fraser also wore a swimsuit for her races that was not the official Speedo-provided suit. Fraser's decision to not wear the official suit hinged on her desire to wear something that fit more comfortably.

Due to the incidents, the heads of Australian Swimming imposed a 10-year ban on Fraser, a decision that led to her retirement. While the ban was lifted before the 1968 Olympics, Fraser did not have time to properly prepare for a fourth Olympiad and another defense of her 100 freestyle crown. "I actually took them to court when I got back from my honeymoon, and we'd won the court case, and the ban had to be lifted straight away," Fraser said.

> But it wasn't in time for me to train for Mexico City, because it was 18 months before Mexico, and I wasn't allowed to swim in any swimming pool where there were other swimmers because I was banned. It would've meant that they would've been banned for life, too, so I couldn't take that opportunity of getting anyone else into trouble. You know, I was the one that got myself into trouble, and I didn't want anyone else to get into trouble.

A 1965 inductee into the International Swimming Hall of Fame, Fraser finished her career with eight Olympic medals—four gold and four silver, including a second-place finish in the 400 freestyle in 1956. She was also the first person to break 1:02, 1:01, 1:00, and the 59-second barrier in the 100 freestyle, and her world record of 58.9 from early in the 1964 season lasted for almost 8 years. Had the 200 freestyle been an Olympic event during Fraser's era, her medal total would undoubtedly be higher, considering that Fraser was a world-record holder in the event.

Nonetheless, Fraser is an icon of her sport and will forever be remembered for making history in the 100 freestyle as the first individual to win gold in an event at three consecutive Olympiads. Fifty years later, Fraser doesn't have trouble recalling her special moment.

"I can remember precisely what I said," Fraser stated of the conclusion of the 100 freestyle in Tokyo. "I said to myself, 'Thank God that's over.'"

4

Meyer's Gold Mine

More than 40 years after competing at the 1968 Games in Mexico City, the United States' Debbie Meyer remains the only individual in Olympic history to win gold medals in three freestyle events in the same Olympiad.

A study of the 1968 Olympics in Mexico City typically produces three standout moments. There was the effect of the altitude, which at more than 7,000 feet contributed to breathing and endurance issues for the athletes. There was the political statement made by Tommie Smith and John Carlos during the medal ceremony for the 200-meter dash, with the track athletes raising black-gloved fists to raise awareness of human rights, particularly those of the black race. There was the flight of Bob Beamon, whose long jump of more than 29 feet broke the world record by nearly 2 feet and endured as the global standard for more than two decades.

Overshadowed in Mexico City was the story of a teenage girl who achieved a feat in the pool that had never before been accomplished and has never since been matched. No, Debbie Meyer did not receive the same attention as the elevation of the host city nor the same hype as members of the American track-and-field squad. Those in swimming circles, however, have a deep appreciation for Meyer, considered a legend in the distance events.

By the time that she was a 14-year-old, Meyer was a major factor on the international scene. She had broken world records in the 400, 800, and 1500 freestyle, and the buzz concerning her talent could not be slowed. As the latest in a long line of young girls to emerge as aquatic superstars, Meyer was viewed as a leading hope for American success at the 1968 Games. Those expectations only grew when Meyer won a pair of gold medals at the 1967 Pan American Championships and continued to break world records.

Still, it's one thing to be surrounded by hype and quite another to perform under the pressure. For Meyer, there was never a sign of strain linked to the lofty predictions attached to her name. She simply went about her business as a fun-

15

loving teenager and star athlete. At the 1968 Olympic Trials, Meyer set world records in the 200, 400, and 800 freestyle, making her an overwhelming favorite to prevail in Mexico City.

Trained by Sherman Chavoor at the Arden Hills Swim Club in California, Meyer had a happy-go-lucky demeanor about her, a personality that was highlighted in numerous newspaper and magazine articles, including a *Sports Illustrated* profile. Sure, Meyer was aware of her status as a world-record holder and the woman to beat at the 1968 Games, but she handled her position with aplomb. "There are a lot of girls who'd love to beat me," she said. "That puts pressure on me. But I just try to stay calm and set goals for myself."

The emergence of Meyer as a star coincided with a favorable change for the youngster in the Olympic swimming schedule. The 1968 Games marked the first time that the 200 and 800 freestyles were part of the women's program, consequently providing Meyer with an opportunity to showcase her range. Before 1968, female swimmers were limited to the 100 and 400 freestyles, a minimized schedule that surely denied a few of Meyer's predecessors the chance to bolster their gold medal totals—Martha Norelius, Helene Madison, Lorraine Crapp, and Dawn Fraser, in particular.

A 16-year-old student at Rio Americano High School in Sacramento, California, when the 1968 Games were held, Meyer may have found the high altitude of Mexico City an advantage. As an asthmatic, Meyer was familiar with enduring practices or races with breathing problems. In the thin air of Mexico City, her rivals came to understand how difficult it can be to compete in top form when oxygen debt is a factor.

Meyer was a focal point from the start. She opened with a convincing victory in the 400 freestyle in 4:31.8, almost 4 seconds clear of her American teammate Linda Gustavson. Meyer then followed with a half-second triumph over fellow American Jan Henne in the 200 freestyle, a win that set the stage for a run at history.

But before Meyer got the chance to contest the 800 freestyle and become the first individual—male or female—to win a gold medal in three freestyle events at the same Olympics, she was hit hard by a stomach bug. For a few days, Meyer was in bad shape, a case of Montezuma's revenge keeping her close to a bathroom. But she was not going to miss the 800 freestyle due to illness, and she went to work in less-than-prime condition.

After winning her 800 freestyle preliminary, Meyer turned up the pace in the championship final, recording a winning time of 9:24.0, more than 11 seconds quicker than silver medalist Pam Kruse of the United States. Speaking of his pupil's dominance in Mexico City, Chavoor said, "I still get goose bumps when I think about it. She was a hell of an athlete. She was in a class by herself."

In less than a week, Meyer made history and was viewed as the queen of her sport. Had she come along in a different era, Meyer could have cashed in on her fame. Nonetheless, she was pleased with what she achieved. "I wasn't into it for the monetary reasons," Meyer said. "I was interested in swimming, working out, traveling, making friends and setting challenges."

Following her Olympic excellence, Meyer returned to training, her sights set on pursuing additional gold medals at the 1972 Olympic Games in Munich. With world records in the 400 and 1500 freestyles following her exploits in Mexico City, there was reason to believe that Meyer had the ability to add to her medal collection, even if Australia's Shane Gould was a fast-rising star.

But at the beginning of 1972, Meyer decided that she was done. She didn't possess the same passion and desire that catapulted her to unprecedented success in 1968. Whether she would have enhanced her Olympic portfolio will remain a mystery, although it was clear that she had improved since her first Olympic foray.

"At first I wanted to repeat in the 200, 400 and 800," she said.

> But I made up my mind to quit on January 8, 1972. The practices weren't fun anymore and had become drudgery. I knew the time had come for me to hang up my suit. My times were still competitive, but I can't say how I might have done. There was a lot more competition in 1972. East Germany was just picking up and there was Shane Gould from Australia.

In assessing her chances at the 1972 Games, Meyer took the humble route. Chavoor, who coached Mark Spitz to seven gold medals in Munich, had a different viewpoint. He did, however, understand Meyer's reasoning for walking away. "She would have won," Chavoor said. "But the motivation was gone. At 16, she had hit the highest peak of any swimmer ever. She had reached the top."

The achievements from Meyer's career are numerous. In addition to her Olympic trifecta, still waiting to be matched, she established a total of 15 world records over four events and became the first woman to break the 18-minute barrier in the 1500 freestyle. In 1968, she became the youngest winner of the James E. Sullivan Award, annually presented to the premier amateur athlete in the United States, and in 1977, she was inducted into the International Swimming Hall of Fame.

"I don't think there's any one thing [which stands out about my career]. I think just the total package," Meyer said. "I loved every minute of it, even the days when I hated working out. I've had great memories. I just hope I can keep them fresh."

5

Seven for Spitz

During the 1972 Games in Munich, Mark Spitz and his iconic mustache wowed the sporting world with a performance for the ages. Spitz won seven gold medals, all in world-record time, and became the sport's measuring stick for greatness for more than three decades.

The mustache. The confident, if not cocky, look. The chiseled physique. All are standout characteristics of Mark Spitz. Once the most revered athlete on the planet, Spitz remains an iconic figure in the sporting world. Even today, more than 40 years after he emerged as the star attraction at the 1972 Olympics in Munich, Spitz's image is easily identifiable.

Success at the Olympic Games can make a career, forever defining an athlete. It's why the mere mention of Jesse, Nadia, and Carl means Owens, Comaneci, and Lewis. But what Mark Spitz accomplished in Munich was entirely different from anything seen before and why he stood alone on an Olympic pedestal until a fellow swimmer came along and knocked him off his lofty perch.

For one week, Spitz could do nothing wrong. He competed in seven finals at the 1972 Games and won seven gold medals, with none of the events featuring much of a scare. All seven of his victories arrived in world-record time, and Spitz left West Germany as a legend and for a whirlwind tour that celebrated his thrilling performance. Truthfully, Spitz accomplished what many expected, but it was also a measure of redemption for what took place 4 years earlier in Mexico City.

On the surface, the two gold medals, one silver, and one bronze that Spitz won at the 1968 Games seemed like a success. After all, few athletes leave an Olympiad with four medals. But there were much higher expectations for Spitz, from outside sources and on a personal level. As a multitime world-record setter, Spitz brashly predicted that he would win six gold medals in his first Olympiad. Obviously, he fell well short of his forecast.

While Spitz won gold medals as a member of the U.S. 400 and 800 freestyle relays, he came up short elsewhere. As the world-record holder in the 100 butterfly, Spitz took the silver medal behind American teammate Doug Russell, a setback that also denied Spitz a place on the 400 medley relay, for which the United States went on to win the gold medal. Spitz also "settled" for the bronze medal in the 100 freestyle, an event in which he became the world-record holder by 1970.

The biggest disappointment and most embarrassing moment of Spitz's Olympiad unfolded in the 200 butterfly. Entering the 1968 Olympics, Spitz had twice set the world record in the event and was viewed as unbeatable in what is one of the sport's most grueling events. But Spitz flopped in the final. As teammates Carl Robie and John Ferris picked up the gold and bronze medals, Spitz finished last, almost 2 seconds behind the seventh-place finisher and an inexplicable 8 seconds off his world-record time.

"I had a difficult time from the 1968 Olympic Games in Mexico City where I was expected to win a lot of gold medals," Spitz said.

And if I just look at my performance of winning two gold, a silver and a bronze, I mean that is pretty remarkable. But the problem was, is that I didn't win a gold medal in two events I held a world record in. And that was just the reason that I basically had this fire in my system to be able to want to actually go for another four years. I found it kind of difficult to work out and train. But I had a focus and the focus was to do the best I could.

If there were any doubts whether Spitz would bounce back following his Mexico City struggles, they were quickly answered. Originally coached by Sherm Chavoor of the Arden Hills Swim Club in California, Spitz joined forces with legendary coach James "Doc" Counsilman when he enrolled at Indiana University following the 1968 Games. As a member of a Hoosiers squad stacked with talent, Spitz did not waste much time returning to form, setting world records over several disciplines.

As he guided Indiana to NCAA team championships, Spitz shifted his focus to the 1972 Games in Munich and atoning for what took place in Mexico City. He studied his competition and adopted a mentality of invincibility, a different approach from what he took into the 1968 Games as a cocky 18-year-old. This time around, Spitz looked at each event on an individual basis, not caught up in the overall medal haul. If he took care of business event by event, the sum would be what he envisioned as possible.

"I think what a true champion has is the ability to be able to know his competitors and everything about his competition, and then try to make one or two less mistakes than those he competes against," Spitz said.

And on a regular basis that they do that, quantitatively saying is that he may have only been four or five percent better than anybody, but since it was always four or five percent better than anybody, the illusion was he was so grand, and that's what makes a great champion.

And [then] they're able to repeat that time and again, regardless of the conditions. Because not every time you come to a swimming pool do you feel great, or if you're in track and field, not every time you hit that track you feel good. Or in boxing, I knew Muhammad Ali. There were a lot of times that he felt terrible. But he knew he had to rise to the occasion. And they did.

Spitz knew the feeling.

If there was any lingering doubt attached to his performance from the 1968 Olympics, Spitz put that notion to rest with immediacy. His first event in Munich was the 200 butterfly, the discipline that produced his last-place finish from 4 years earlier. Really, it was the perfect way for Spitz to erase any demons.

Climbing the blocks on August 28 as the world-record holder, as was the case in 1968, Spitz did not have any trouble this time around. He bolted to the front of the field and buried his competition behind a world-record time of 2:00.70. The United States swept the medals, but silver medalist Gary Hall (2:02.86) and bronze medalist Robin Backhaus (2:03.23) may as well have competed in a different race. About 40 minutes later, Spitz added his second gold medal and world record when he anchored a squad of David Edgar, John Murphy, and Jerry Heidenreich to a 3-second rout of the Soviet Union in the 400 freestyle relay.

As Spitz started his Olympic program, he was equally known for the mustache that he refused to shave. While other athletes were intent on shaving all hair from their bodies, Spitz went for an antiswimmer look, not concerned that the facial hair would cost him a few hundredths of a second here or a few hundredths of a second there. The mustache also proved to be an advantage from a mental standpoint, as his competition was consumed with its presence. Several swimmers from the Soviet Union asked Spitz whether it slowed him down. A year later, after they saw what Spitz accomplished, many of the Soviet swimmers sported mustaches of their own.

"I grew that mustache out of spite because my college coach said you need to look like the all-American boy," Spitz said. "It took me about five or six months to grow that mustache. I went to the Olympic Trials and had intentions of shaving it off. All my competitors in the press were talking about it. I go, 'Wow, they're not figuring out how to beat me. I might as well keep this thing.'"

With his first two victories supplying momentum, Spitz secured his third gold medal with a victory in the 200 freestyle, overhauling teammate Steve Genter in the latter stages of the race and via another world-record effort. Standing on the podium to receive his gold medal, Spitz placed a pair of Adidas sneakers behind him. After the playing of the "Star Spangled Banner," Spitz picked up the shoes and acknowledged the crowd by raising his arms. The Soviet Union claimed that Spitz was advertising for Adidas and consequently violating the Olympics' rule of amateurism. The International Olympic Committee looked into the incident but cleared Spitz of any wrongdoing. It was clear that if Spitz couldn't be beaten in the pool, opponents would try to find a loophole to eliminate their biggest obstacle. "I'm already a Jesse Owens," Spitz kidded. "Now they're trying to make a Jim Thorpe out of me."

Spitz was referring to the fact that he already had the success of Owens, who won four gold medals in track and field at the 1936 Olympics, but was being attacked like Thorpe. A gold medalist in the pentathlon and decathlon at the 1912 Olympics in Stockholm, Thorpe had his medals revoked by the International Olympic Committee because he was briefly paid as a professional baseball player (the medals were restored years later, after Thorpe's death).

Spitz's fourth and fifth medals (and world records) were earned on August 31 when he prevailed in the 100 butterfly and as a member of the 800 freestyle relay. Spitz had no problem in either event, winning by more than a second over Canadian Bruce Robertson in the 100 butterfly and by 6 seconds with his teammates over West Germany in the 800 freestyle relay.

As Spitz rolled through his program, the pressure that he felt at the beginning of the Games largely eased. Still, he had some concern over his final individual event, the 100 freestyle. Spitz was beginning to feel weary from his demanding schedule, and he knew that Heidenreich would bring a challenge, along with defending champion Michael Wenden of Australia. At one point, the possibility of withdrawing crossed his mind.

"Each day that I swam and I won a gold medal, it was like one brick shy of a load getting off of the cart," Spitz said.

And so, I felt that I was actually having a better go of it. But I was exhausted by the time it came to my last individual event, the 100-meter freestyle. And I have to say that the last stroke that I took at the Olympic Games, I don't think I could have taken another stroke. I was 100 percent up until the last stroke, and I literally had one drop of gas in my tank at the end of that. So thank goodness it ended.

Spitz surged at the start of the 100 freestyle, a tactic that surprised Heidenreich, who expected Spitz to save some energy for the latter half of the race. While Heidenreich closed the gap on his teammate over the last lap, he fell short of catching Spitz, who set a world record of 51.22, ahead of the 51.65 by Heidenreich. Wenden proved to be a nonfactor, finishing fifth.

For Spitz, his final day in the pool was primarily a formality. He picked up his seventh gold medal with ease, handling the butterfly leg of the 400 medley relay. The team of Mike Stamm, Tom Bruce, Spitz, and Heidenreich was timed in 3:48.16, 4 seconds clear of East Germany. For Spitz, the end featured a combination of jubilation and relief.

After the relay, Spitz's teammates carried him around the deck for a well-deserved victory lap. It is a moment that Spitz has never forgotten. "That picture with my teammates holding me high above them I enjoy more than the one that was taken with the seven gold medals around my neck," he said. "Having a tribute from your teammates is a feeling that can never be duplicated."

Spitz's achievement figured to be the talk of the remainder of the Olympics, but in the early hours of September 5, only several hours after Spitz completed his perfect week, the terrorist group Black September took 11 members of the Israeli Olympic delegation hostage. A faction of the Palestine Liberation Organization, Black September broke into the building holding the Israeli athletes and coaches and used deadly force in the hostage taking.

When Spitz woke the next morning and made his way to a final press conference, he was unaware of what was unfolding. Soon, he was clued in on the details, and because of his Jewish religion, officials informed Spitz that he would be ushered out of Munich. By 5 o'clock at night, Spitz was in a car, an army blanket draped over his head, and taken to the airport for a flight to London. Ultimately, negotiations between German police and government officials failed, and the 11 Israeli hostages were killed, along with five of the eight Palestinian terrorists. The Games went from being a joyous occasion to a somber event.

"It was terrible. I mean, you know, the Olympic Games today is modeled based on the security not only for the athletes, but for the press, the media, the spectators, and the citizens of a host city," Spitz said.

> And the International Olympic Committee has done a great job over the years to protect everybody. But it's totally different. Here I became a real gigantic event as a sports celebrity winning seven gold medals. Then it became a news event. And then all of a sudden it became a tragedy. And then it became elevated at a much higher level, and we're talking about it right now, 40 years later.

Although Spitz retired after the Munich Games, his name has remained a constant in the sport. Anytime a multievent talent comes along, comparisons to Spitz are made, even if they are a stretch. Really, it wasn't until the mid-1980s when a legitimate comparison surfaced, thanks to the talent of Matt Biondi.

Like Spitz, Biondi raced the freestyle-butterfly combination and embraced a program that featured seven events. In the lead-up to the 1988 Olympics in Seoul, Biondi could not escape Spitz's shadow. Never did an interview end without Biondi being asked about matching Spitz's seven gold medals, despite Biondi never once suggesting that it was a goal.

"I don't feel it's a fair comparison," said Biondi's coach, Nort Thornton, of the Spitz comparisons.

> But people are going to do it. You can't stop them. It's unfortunate people get compared, but that's human nature. The rules have changed, and people can't swim as many events as they were able to in 1972. There are certain comparisons like the speed they both travel through the water, but Matt is definitely not Mark. He is his own swimmer. Someday people will be comparing another young swimmer to Matt. That's the way it works.

Biondi enjoyed a sterling showing at the Seoul Games, leaving with five gold medals, a silver, and a bronze. As impressive as he was, Biondi was actually painted as a failure by some media outlets. The same scenario befell Michael Phelps in 2004, when he became the latest American star to hear the Spitz comparisons.

An Olympian as a 15-year-old in 2000, Phelps started to show his versatility a couple of years later, namely at the 2002 U.S. National Championships. There, Phelps won the 100 butterfly, 200 butterfly, 200 individual medley, and 400 individual medley, victories that were complemented by a third-place finish in the 200 freestyle. It was a week that got the wheels turning in the head of Bob Bowman, Phelps's coach.

"I thought that Michael could do a lot of stuff, but it was then that I thought about Spitz's record and told myself, 'Wow, he can really do this,'" Bowman said of the 2002 National Championships. "That was in the back of my mind, but I still didn't want to think about seven medals. The way to think about seven medals isn't to talk about it, it's to train. When we left that meet, we knew at the least, that Michael was going to be our Ian Thorpe."

When Phelps came back from the next year's World Championships with six medals, the Spitz talk was in full effect. And when it was announced that Phelps would contest eight events at the 2004 Olympics in Athens, Phelps had no chance of turning back the Spitz queries. Trained by his management group at Octagon Sports, Phelps knew exactly how to handle the Spitz questions.

"Records are always made to be broken no matter what they are. Anybody can do anything they set their mind to," Phelps said.

> I've said it all along. I want to be the first Michael Phelps, not the second Mark Spitz. Never once will I ever downplay his accomplishment and what he did. It's still an amazing feat and will always be an amazing accomplishment in the swimming world and the Olympics.
>
> To have something like that to shoot for, it made those days when you were tired and didn't want to be [at practice] and just wanted to go home and sleep, it made those days easier to be able to look at him and say, "I want to do this." It's something that I've wanted to do, and I'm thankful for having him do what he did.

Phelps's first attempt at Spitz's standard came up short in Athens, but the effort was nothing short of spectacular. Competing against deeper competition than Spitz's and forced to handle a more arduous schedule, Phelps won six gold medals and two bronze medals. Like Biondi, Phelps was still called a failure in some circles.

Four years later, there was nothing but awe. At the 2008 Games in Beijing, Phelps was a perfect eight-for-eight and moved ahead of Spitz as the greatest athlete in a single Olympiad. Phelps needed a couple of miracles along the way, notably a come-from-behind anchor leg by Jason Lezak in the 400 freestyle relay and a fingernail triumph over Serbian Milorad Cavic in the 100 butterfly. But Phelps got the job done and became the new measuring stick for Olympic greatness.

During Phelps's emergence as a global superstar, Spitz was difficult to read. At times, he seemed gracious and respectful toward Phelps's talent. At other times, he seemed jealous. "I set a record that lasted 36 years until Michael Phelps broke it," Spitz said. "It's amazing that I was an inspiration to someone not even born yet to achieve and excel in my sport. That's the greatest accolade I could leave for my sport and the Olympic movement. What is a higher regard?"

Yes, four decades have passed since Mark Spitz wowed the sporting world with what was then the finest performance in Olympic history. While his seven-gold effort has since been surpassed, Spitz's legacy is going nowhere. He will always remain a legend, with what he produced in 1972 a special showing.

CHART NO. 5.1

At the 1972 Olympics in Munich, Mark Spitz produced the greatest Olympic performance to date, winning seven gold medals and setting as many world records. Spitz's effort stood as the Olympic standard of excellence until the 2008 Games in Beijing, when Michael Phelps won eight gold medals, including seven world records. Here's a look at Spitz's performances from Munich:

Event	Winning Time	Margin of Victory
Freestyle		
100	51.22	0.43
200	1:52.78	0.95
Butterfly		
100	54.27	1.29
200	2:00.70	2.16
Freestyle relay		
400	3:26.42	3.30
800	7:35.78	5.91
Medley relay		
400	3:48.16	4.10

6

Hello and Goodbye

The career of Australian Shane Gould was brief, lasting just one Olympiad and not stretching beyond her teenage years. But before she left the sport, Gould won five individual medals at the 1972 Games in Munich, a feat that remains unmatched by another female. Her legacy short, it still remains powerful.

How great could she have been? Could she have posted an Olympic medal count that reached double figures? Could she have continued to improve? Or did we see the best that we were going to see? Could she have been capable of turning back the East German doping machine, which emerged just after her retirement? Or, like many others, would she have fallen victim to drug-fueled opposition?

These are just a few questions that spring to mind when contemplating the brief, yet prosperous, career of Australian Shane Gould. In a flash, or so it seemed, Gould emerged on the international scene as a special talent. Just as quickly, she was gone from the sport, on her own accord, leaving many to wonder about what could have been.

Burnout is a term largely used in negative fashion, particularly when connected to the sports world. Simply, it describes athletes who hit their peak—usually at an early age—and then leave their sport or experience a rapid fall from grace. It comes in a variety of forms, including the too-much, too-soon genre, in which an athlete goes from rags to riches in a blink but does not know how to handle the drastic change in lifestyle. There is also the need-something-else type, in which an athlete grows tired of his or her sport and flees the playing surface to see what opportunities exist outside the bubble in which he or she has primarily resided.

However, the most common form of burnout results from athletes' inability to handle the immense pressure placed on their shoulders while living a life under the constant glare of the public eye. It is this type of burnout that caused the tennis careers of Tracy Austin and Andrea Jaeger to fizzle out. It is this type of burnout, too, that got the best of Shane Gould.

Early-teen success is not uncommon in the sport of swimming. While it is rare for male athletes to bloom at a young age—with a few exceptions, including a guy named Michael Phelps—there are numerous examples of female excellence during early teenage years. Some of the biggest names in swimming history fit that description, such as Tracy Caulkins and Janet Evans. Gould came before either of those women.

When Gould came to train under Forbes Carlile, the legendary and innovative Australian coach, it did not take long for Carlile to set in motion a game plan that would lead Gould to considerable success. He knew a vast talent when he saw one, and Carlile instantly came to the understanding that Gould could be special, likely capable of accomplishing feats never before seen.

Carlile's beliefs about Gould's potential were not steeped in hyperbole, either. After World War II, Carlile became the premier coach in Australia and one of the most respected in the world, a man who guided several athletes to Olympic success and earned coaching appointments to the Olympic Games. More, he brought innovation to the sport in the form of interval training, pace clocks, and heart-rate measurement.

"She was very good when she came to us," Carlile said of Gould.

> She was a 12- or 13-year-old that had done well. As a matter of fact, when she first got into the pool with us, it was a question of when she'd break Dawn Fraser's record, not if she'd break it. We trained her as an endurance athlete, and it carried her through, both in sprints and in distances. That was a new idea.

Although Gould started to surface as a potential superstar upon joining forces with Carlile, the year 1971 proved to be the launching pad of what would be a scintillating yet brief reign. The year before the Olympic Games is largely considered a groundwork campaign, a period in which the headliners of the next Olympiad truly emerge. Almost on cue, Gould jumped into the spotlight with a number of sterling performances.

By the time that Gould arrived for the Santa Clara International Invitational in California in the summer of 1971, Gould already had a pair of world records to her name. A few months earlier, while competing in London, Gould tied the global mark of the legendary Dawn Fraser in the 100 freestyle, then set a world record in the 200 freestyle. Her career was surging and took off even more when she notched a world record in the 400 freestyle in Santa Clara. Suddenly, Gould wasn't just an Australian hopeful but a focal point of the upcoming Olympic Games in Munich. Her confidence, too, was soaring, as were the expectations—internal and external. "I'm pretty sure I'll get a record here," Gould said upon her arrival in Santa Clara. "I seem to improve every time I get in the water. I haven't finished a race yet where I felt I couldn't go a bit further."

By the end of 1971, the swimming world was in a full froth over what Gould could pull off at the Munich Games. In an unprecedented feat, Gould held every world record from the 100 freestyle through the 1500 freestyle, with the 200, 400, and 800 distances connecting both ends of the range. She was as much a sprinter as a distance performer, a combination that just wasn't known. Gould somehow possessed the fast-twitch fibers necessary in sprinting and the endurance required to handle the grueling nature of the distance events.

Known for the two-beat kick pioneered by Carlile, Gould was viewed as a multimedal hopeful in Munich. There was little doubt that she would reach the podium on several occasions, but how many would be gold? "If Shane Gould remains in form, her mother may require the help of a full-time gardener," wrote Jerry Kirshenbaum in a *Sports Illustrated* feature six months before the Munich Olympics.

To hear Australians discuss the matter, Shane is a cinch to win anywhere from four to seven gold medals when she gets her teeth into this summer's Olympics. If they are right, the Aussies could enjoy their best showing since they took eight of 13 swimming gold medals at the 1956 Olympics in Melbourne.

As the 1972 Games approached, the pressure on Gould was heightening with each passing day. Only the presence of Mark Spitz—the American who went on to win seven gold medals and become a global icon—kept Gould from presumably being the featured athlete of Munich. Regardless, Gould was watched closely.

With the 1500 freestyle a non-Olympic event for women at the Olympic Games, Gould was expected to contest four individual events at the Olympics: the 100, 200, 400, and 800 freestyles. Two relays were also supposed to be on the agenda. But thanks to the prompting of Carlile, who had witnessed great strides by Gould in the nonfreestyle strokes, Carlile was able to convince his pupil to add the 200 individual medley to her agenda. It proved to be a wise decision, as the event produced the first gold medal for the 15-year-old, along with a world record of 2:23.07, a time that was a half second clear of East Germany's Kornelia Ender.

Two other gold medals followed for Gould—one in the 200 freestyle and the other in the 400 freestyle. Over the shorter distance, Gould powered through her four laps in 2:03.56, a time that provided a win by almost a second over American Shirley Babashoff. Making the decision even more impressive was the fact that Gould took a second and a half off Babashoff's world record, set at the U.S. Olympic Trials. The 400 freestyle, too, was dominant. Gould's world record of 4:19.04 gave the teen sensation a 3-second-plus cushion over silver medalist Novella Calligaris of Italy.

But with all the hype surrounding her exploits heading to Munich, there was disappointment when Gould failed to win gold medals in the 100 and 800 freestyles, events in which she was also the world-record holder. Part of the problem, so went the speculation, was Gould's awareness of the expectations.

In the 100 freestyle, which figured to be a certain victory, Gould settled for the bronze medal behind Americans Sandy Neilson and Babashoff. Her time was more than a second slower than her world record and did not match the high level of her efforts in other events. Stretching up to the 800 freestyle, Gould again found herself beaten by an American, this time Keena Rothhammer.

Most times, Gould would have been revered for her aquatic excellence. But competing in the same pool as Spitz left the Australian in a no-win situation. "Gould was spectacular," Kirshenbaum wrote in *Sports Illustrated*. "But Mark the Shark was much more so, and swim buffs will be recounting his feats in Munich for as long as pools make waves."

If Gould was overlooked in Munich, history has taught us that her achievements in 1972 deserved greater appreciation. It wasn't until the 2008 Games in Beijing in which Gould's haul of five individual medals was matched by a swimmer, and it took Michael Phelps's other-worldly performance of eight gold medals to do the trick—five individual and three in relay duty.

For her gender, though, Gould remains alone, the only woman to earn a place on five individual-event podiums in a single Olympiad. Had the Australian women been as formidable as in past Games, Gould could have added relay hardware to her collection, too. Alas, Australia performed poorly in the two relays, and Gould's final tally was linked solely to her abilities and not the skills of teammates.

As Gould left Munich, few thought that they had seen the last of her on a major international stage. She was expected to compete the next year at the inaugural FINA World Championships, and given that she would be only 19 at the time, the 1976 Olympics in Montreal figured to be an encore of her initial Olympic foray. None of it was meant to be.

In 1973, as a mere 16-year-old, Gould revealed that she was done with the sport on a competitive basis. In what can only be described as a shocking development, Gould prematurely retired. "There's a whole series of things that happened," Gould said of her decision to walk away from the pool.

> I went to America after the Olympics. I was not a happy chappy. I was wondering whether to swim or not to swim and I came back. I had a lot of hot chocolate fudge sundaes and doughnuts, and didn't swim as much, so I just blew up like a balloon, and that's not very good for competition swimming to be overweight. And I was just confused. There was a lot of pressure for me to stay swimming, and I really had no goals to work toward, and just in the confusion of it all, I just had to run away.

When Gould left the sport in 1973, her decision coincided with the time when the East German women began to flourish, primarily due to the implementation of a systematic doping program, which raised performance levels across the board. Ahead of her time, Gould's performances suddenly looked ordinary next to the records set by the East Germans, including Ender.

Had she stayed around, what could Gould have done? Would she have continued to improve, lowering her times in a variety of events? Considering that she set a world record in early 1973 in the 1500 freestyle, there is no reason to believe that she would have slowed down. Meanwhile, could Gould have been an athlete capable of turning back the East Germans and their doped-up bodies? The questions abound, but there will never be any definitive answers.

What we do know is that Shane Gould, as brief as her stardom was, ranks among the elite performers in the sport's history. More, what she managed to produce at the 1972 Olympic Games remains historic, unmatched by any other female despite 40 years of attempts. It is a reason why Gould continues to be used as a measuring stick for greatness.

7

A Matter of Timing

If the epic 400 individual medley race from the 1972 Olympics between Sweden's Gunnar Larsson and the United States' Tim McKee were held today, both men would own gold medals. Instead, Larsson is the only man who owns the pinnacle of Olympic achievement, with the timing rules of the day playing in his favor.

The 400 individual medley is arguably the most grueling event in the sport. Some might argue for the 1500 freestyle or the 200 butterfly, but it's a splitting-hairs situation when discussing any of these disciplines. The fact is the 400 individual medley is a grind, more than 4 minutes of pain spread over the four competitive strokes.

Pacing the event is of utmost importance, along with knowing when to pressure the gas pedal just a little bit more. By the time an athlete is done, a swimmer will have completed 100 meters each of butterfly, backstroke, breaststroke, and freestyle, expending so much energy that the lungs burn and every muscle aches. Some events—the shorter distances in particular—can be faked, with swimmers able to grind through them by relying on talent alone. There is no negotiation with the 400 individual medley. It makes no deals. Try to deceive it, and the athlete is sure to receive a swift backhand of humility.

So, imagine being American Tim McKee. At the 1972 Olympic Games in Munich, McKee swam a time in the 400 individual medley identical—by today's standards—to the winning mark produced by Sweden's Gunnar Larsson. Yet, only Larsson stood on the top step of the medals podium, with McKee left to polish a piece of silver.

How did it happen? It's one of the great stories of Olympic lore, even if it is grossly overshadowed by other events that transpired in Germany.

The 1972 Games in Munich will forever be remembered for what Mark Spitz managed to accomplish. Inside the Schwimmhalle, Spitz was perfect in his seven events, capturing gold medals and setting world records in each of his disciplines.

The effort stood as the hallmark of the sport until Michael Phelps came along and fittingly went eight-for-eight at the 2008 Olympics in Beijing.

The Munich Olympics, too, will be recalled for the tragic events in which 11 members of the Israeli contingent were killed in a hostage-taking movement by the Palestinian terrorist group Black September. The Games will also be remembered for the officiating calamity that handed the Soviet Union the gold medal over the United States on the basketball court. Still, there is something unique about the clash between Larsson and McKee.

As speculation concerning the swimming competition ramped up for the Munich Games, Larsson and McKee found themselves viewed through different lenses. Larsson was the known commodity: an Olympian in 1968 in multiple events, a European champion, and a world-record setter. McKee, meanwhile, was an off-the-map type. Initially not expected to qualify for the Olympic Games, McKee managed to nail down berths in both individual medley disciplines and the 200 backstroke. Still, he hovered in the shadows of his more-established teammates, especially Gary Hall Sr. in the medley events.

As the reigning world-record holder from the U.S. Trials, Hall was the heavy favorite to win the 400 individual medley. Although Larsson boasted an impressive resume and Hungarian Andras Hargitay was a rising force from the junior ranks, Hall's world mark was dominant and represented a gap that seemed impossible to close.

So, when the 400 individual medley started, it was hardly shocking to see Hall bolt to the front of the field and open up a considerable lead. With his best strokes in the first half of the medley, Hall was nearly three body lengths ahead after the butterfly leg and enjoyed a full three-length advantage after the backstroke leg. That's when the race got interesting and began its climactic surge toward becoming a historic moment in the sport.

As the swimmers moved into the third leg, the breaststroke, Hall encountered problems. Not only was the breaststroke his worst stroke by a significant margin, he was clearly laboring and fading. Hall's struggles were capitalized on by Larsson, McKee, and Hargitay, whose balance in the event allowed them to reel in the favorite.

By the 275-meter mark, McKee had caught Hall, and it was only a matter of time before Larsson passed Hall, too. By 325 meters, Larsson was leading the field, with McKee squarely in the mix. Over the last 75 meters of freestyle, it was going to be a stellar duel between the Swede and the American, uncertainty reigning over who would prevail. Stunningly, the uncertainty remained after both men finished.

When Larsson touched the wall and looked to the scoreboard, he saw a time of 4:31.98 and a "1" by his name, the numeral signifying his place in the race. When McKee touched the wall and looked to the scoreboard, he saw a time of 4:31.98 and a "1" by his name. Each man was under the impression that he had prevailed in the biggest race of his career. Hargitay was the only medalist who instantly knew his standing, as he took bronze ahead of American Steve Furniss, with Hall a disappointing fifth.

"That whole last leg, I knew I had it won," McKee said. "Then when I touched and saw Larsson, I didn't think I'd won. When I saw a one next to my name on the scoreboard, I thought I'd won again, but 15 seconds later, I saw the one next to his name. Then I didn't know what was going on."

Similar confusion encompassed Larsson, who had a brief discussion with his countryman Bengt Gingsjo about the finish. "I looked up at the scoreboard after I finished and saw the one, after my time, and I was just so happy that I won," Larsson said. "Then the Swedish guy in Lane Three asked me who won and I said, 'I did,' and he goes, 'no you didn't, there's another one up there.'"

The drama concerning the true gold medalist was not settled for several minutes as officials convened and discussed the outcome. Eventually, they returned with the realization that the timing system could measure the finish to the thousandth of a second, and using that option showed Larsson prevailed 4:31.981 to 4:31.983. That difference in time is significantly faster than the blink of an eye and represents a physical distance thinner than a coat of paint. Upon learning of his victory, Larsson and the Swedish contingent broke into a celebration.

For McKee, the silver medal was tough to accept. He couldn't help but pinpoint a moment in the race in which he made a tactical error, a mistake that he was convinced cost him the gold medal. "With 20 meters to go, I looked around and that messed up my stroke for two or three turns," McKee said. "Normally, that wouldn't matter, but I know it cost me two-thousandths of a second. There has to be a winner and a loser, even if it's two-millionths."

The precedent set by the duel between Larsson and McKee resulted in officials deciding that any future ties would not be taken out to the thousandth of a second. Obviously, that decision provided no solace for McKee, who saw the rule book of FINA, the sport's governing body, altered to read as part of Section SW 11.2:

> When automatic equipment is used, the results shall be recorded only to 1/100 of a second. When timing to 1/1000 of a second is available, the third digit shall not be recorded or used to determine time or placement. In the event of equal times, all swimmers who have recorded the same time at 1/100 of a second shall be accorded the same placing. Times displayed on the electronic scoreboard should show only to 1/100 of a second.

The decision to not move behind hundredths of a second played a role in the outcome of two future Olympic races. At the 1984 Olympics in Los Angeles, Americans Nancy Hogshead and Carrie Steinseifer shared the gold medal in the 100 freestyle after posting matching times of 55.92. Sixteen years later at the 2000 Games in Sydney, United States teammates Gary Hall Jr. and Anthony Ervin each touched the wall in 21.98 in the 50 freestyle.

Without the events of 1972, what could have happened in 1984 and 2000? Could Hogshead have been relegated to the silver medal? Could it have happened to Ervin? Of course, it is an answer that we will never know, largely because McKee—in retrospect—played the role of a guinea pig in an unexpected electronic timing experiment.

The finish between Larsson and McKee in Munich replayed itself in the 200 individual medley a few days later, with Larsson again winning gold ahead of McKee but this time by more than a second. Four years later, at the 1976 Olympics in Montreal, McKee was again the silver medalist in the 400 medley, this time finishing behind American teammate Rod Strachan.

Seven years after his Olympic triumphs, Larsson was inducted into the International Swimming Hall of Fame in 1979. Considering the closeness of their premier battle and his illustrious career of three Olympic silver medals, McKee figured to be inducted not long after, right? Actually, it took until 1998 for McKee to receive induction, proof of just how much weight an Olympic gold medal carries. For McKee, two thousandths of a second seemed to equate a 19-year wait.

Asked about the impact of that finish on his life, McKee had a simple answer; the reply, too, placed perspective on the moment: "It's not who I am," McKee said. "It's who I was and where I've been."

8

Gulping Down Gold

East Germany's female athletes of the 1970s and the 1980s were forced to swallow anabolic steroids to aid their performances. Due to this systematic doping program, many of their competitors were robbed of their rightful place in history while the East German athletes were victimized by health issues and questions of how good they really were.

Statistics do not always portray the truest of stories. They can be manipulated, or those trying to make a point might simply select the figures that benefit their argument. On the football field, time of possession is a statistic that is loved by some and loathed by others, due to the inconsistency of its validity.

In some contests, time of possession can represent the effectiveness of a team in regard to ball control. Yet, in games featuring a quick-strike offense, does it really matter how long a team had the ball? Simply put, the answer is no. It matters only that the team scored.

When it comes to the history of East Germany's stranglehold on women's swimming supremacy in the 1970s and 1980s, though, statistics do not lie. At the 1968 Olympic Games in Mexico City, East German women managed two silver medals and a bronze. At the 1972 Olympics in Munich, East Germany tallied four silver medals and a bronze on the women's side.

Each of the aforementioned medal hauls is ordinary, an illustration of a country with modest success. But when East Germany suddenly surged to major success at the next two versions of the World Championships (1973 and 1975) and then registered victories in 11 of 13 events at the 1976 Olympics in Montreal, it made perfect sense that allegations of performance-enhancing drug use flew, finger-pointing that was later confirmed via documentation.

From 1973 through 1988, a black cloud hung over women's swimming. Although East German athletes passed drug tests, there was little doubt that their success was fueled by factors well beyond traditional training methods. Not only did East German times drastically drop, but the athletes possessed signs of steroid use: enlarged muscles, deep voices, acne-covered skin.

It wasn't until the Berlin Wall fell in 1989 that the systematic doping program instituted by East German sports officials was confirmed. When documents of the Stasi, the East German secret police, were revealed, it was shown that the country designed a strictly organized and elaborate scheme that reached as many as 10,000 athletes spanning multiple sports and required the cooperation of coaches across the country.

Two men were primarily responsible for the implementation of the program. Manfred Ewald was the East German minister of sport from 1961 to 1989 and the head of the East German Olympic Committee from 1973 to 1990. It was Ewald who coordinated the program and who was also involved in the identification of young athletes who would be groomed for sporting success in part through the aid of doping. Meanwhile, Manfred Hoeppner served as East Germany's top sports doctor during the doping regime and was responsible for overseeing the distribution of performance-enhancing drugs and constructing a system that ensured success on the athletic stage but steered clear of being detected by doping officials.

The program developed by Ewald and Hoeppner and supported by the top levels of the East German government relied primarily on the use of the steroid Oral-Turinabol. The drug was typically given in the form of a little blue pill, and it enabled athletes to gain muscle mass and endure grueling training regimens. At times, however, Oral-Turinabol was administered through injections.

The delivery of Oral-Turinabol became a daily routine for the athletes, the majority of which in swimming were teenagers. Initially unaware of the effects of the drug, the athletes were told that it was part of a recovery or rejuvenation program designed to help their bodies bounce back from the heavy workload. The teenage girls at the center of the program had no choice but to accept the pills or find themselves sent home, their careers over for all intents and purposes.

"It was really exhausting," said Rica Reinisch, who won three gold medals at the 1980 Olympics and set four individual world records. "Sometimes you swam until you found your arms were dragging along the bottom of the pool. It was dreadful. We usually got the tablets after very hard water-training sessions. Vitamin C, Vitamin B, potassium, calcium, magnesium, all kinds of pills. It was a real cupful."

Just how effective was the usage of Oral-Turinabol? Well, a deeper look at the numbers recorded by East Germany tells a distinct story. Consider these figures:

- In major international competition from 1973 to 1988, East Germany tallied 65 gold medals, nearly three times the total won by the United States (23).
- During East Germany's drug-fueled reign, its athletes accounted for 131 medals in major international competition, far exceeding the 79 won by the United States.
- Between the 1976 Olympics and 1980 Olympics, East German women won 22 of a possible 26 gold medals and totaled 44 medals of the 78 up for grabs.

- In the final Olympiad of the East German doping era, the country's women won 10 gold medals, 5 silver medals, and 7 bronze medals, with Kristin Otto becoming the first woman to win 6 gold medals in a major international competition.
- From 1973 to 1986, the world record in the 100 freestyle was broken on 14 occasions, all by East German athletes. During that time, the record was lowered from 58.25 to 54.73, an almost unheard of drop. The first 10 records in the run were set by Kornelia Ender, who improved from 58.25 to 55.65 in a matter of only 3 years.

These statistics paint a clear picture of just how potent East Germany was and how potent the performance-enhancing drugs were. While the nation's women were the focal point of the doping program, it was not limited to the female gender. Several male swimmers also benefited, including world champion Jorg Hoffmann, a distance freestyler.

Although the teenage women did not suspect anything amiss when they first started to receive their "vitamins," they started to sense impropriety as they gained muscle and endured deepening voices. Nonetheless, they stayed quiet, in fear of having their careers crushed in an instant. It can be argued, too, that they were brainwashed by their coaches, convinced what they were doing was not wrong.

"The first time was during the Olympic Games, where older athletes were making jokes about it, saying 'oh it's time to go and get our shots.'" Reinisch said of her realization that something was wrong. "And ignorant as I was, I went and refused to have the jab before the [400 medley relay]. And afterward, my coach came and said, 'Rica, either you let them give you the stuff or your four years of training have been for nothing.' That's when I knew that something wasn't right."

Reinisch is one of several former East German swimmers to come forward and recognize that a systematic doping program was in place. Others have suggested that it was a possibility but have stopped short of fully verifying their knowledge. Still, others will not admit—even with Stasi paperwork stating as much—that they were part of a steroid-boosted program.

Upon realizing that her daughter was being given performance-enhancing drugs and experiencing ovarian complications, Reinisch's mother confronted her coach, Uwe Neumann, and expressed disgust with what had taken place. "My mother went to the pool and screamed her head off at Uwe Neumann," Reinisch said. "We weren't even allowed to say what we knew. 'I will rescue my daughter from your clutches.' The swimming pool went dead quiet. Everyone around us was taken aback. That was, so to speak, my last official deed in the swimming pool."

When Otto was flourishing, winning multiple world titles and delivering her Olympic excellence in Seoul, there were numerous allegations of drug use, all of which were rebuffed by Otto and her coaches. When Stasi records were made public, Otto's name was listed among the athletes who received performance-enhancing drugs. Still, she is not the only athlete who has remained in denial or has played coy on the subject.

"Now, after all this time, I still ask myself whether it could be possible they gave me things because I remember being given injections during training and competition, but this was explained to me as being substances to help me regenerate and recuperate," Ender said. "It was natural to think this way because the distance swimmers had more injections than we did as sprinters. It's very sad. The only losers in that are the athletes."

After the fall of the Berlin Wall and the revelation that a systematic doping program was indeed in place, athletes affected by doping filed lawsuits against those who treated them like medical experiments. For many athletes, the effects of Oral-Turinabol use have been devastating, with miscarriages and deformities among offspring being commonplace. Others have suffered from ailments such as cancer and liver damage.

Among those facing suit were Ewald and Hoeppner. While Ewald showed no remorse to the athletes who were lab rats, Hoeppner offered an apology, albeit one that had a caveat. While apologizing, Hoeppner also defended his actions, stating they were in the best interest of the athletes. Not surprisingly, those in the courtroom were stunned that Hoeppner could actually justify what unfolded.

"Many people pop pills in order to maintain their ability to work hard, so where is the real difference between sport and the real world?" Hoeppner said.

> Doctors in the sports-medicine field don't have the opportunity to certify an athlete unfit to work, but the athletes nevertheless ask the doctors to help them maintain their competitive edge. So doctors should not shy away from this question. It is always like walking a tightrope.
>
> According to the 1987 pharmaceutical law, the proper use of drugs includes the prevention of damage. We did scientific studies in the East to prove that it was necessary to use these supporting means, these drugs, for performance. We justified our use of the drugs to prevent damage to the athletes. Even today we have an ongoing discussion about the ethics of using performance enhancement. If the court finds that I am wrong about the use of drugs, then I have to accept this, but 26 years ago, the situation was very different. The objective of supplying pills was to minimize injury and maximize training hours.
>
> I deeply regret that I was not able to protect all athletes from harm. I beg those athletes who suffered ill-health to accept my apologies for this.

Ewald and Hoeppner were found guilty of being accessories to inflicting bodily harm, but their sentence of probation was more a slap on the wrist, especially in the context of the health issues realized by the athletes.

While the East German swimmers were victims of their country's program and their coaches' refusal to do what was right, the rest of the world fell victim from a competitive standpoint. There is little doubt that other athletes of the era used performance-enhancing drugs in pockets but nothing like the systematic setup of East Germany.

As U.S. swimmers climbed the blocks to race against their East German foes, they knew that they were not racing on a level playing field. However, it was viewed as poor form or as a lack of sportsmanship to accuse a rival of doping. Primarily, the allegations were whispered and kept within team circles.

"Prior to the 1976 Olympics, the East Germans had just blown us away in the World Championships," said Jack Nelson, the coach of the U.S. women at the 1976 Games in Montreal. "And our girls were honestly bothered by the fact that they had been the greatest team in the world for a while and then suddenly the East Germans just are blowing us away. We knew while we were there that they were beating up on us with steroids and whatever and there was nothing we could do about it, right? Plus, we didn't want to be the nasty Americans at the Olympics."

The decision to stay quiet and not hurl accusations was not something that American Shirley Babashoff could accept. One of the world's best freestylers, Babashoff knew that her opposition was benefiting from steroid use and that it was robbing her of Olympic gold. At the 1976 Games, Babashoff was the silver medalist in the 200, 400, and 800 freestyles, beaten in all three disciplines by an East German.

Angered by the situation, Babashoff decided to speak out, publicly voicing her belief that the East Germans were winning through illicit means. Her courage to express her concerns was met with denials by the East German camp, and the media immediately presented Babashoff as a sore loser, giving her the moniker "Surly Shirley."

"They had gotten so big, and when we heard their voices, we thought we were in a coed locker room," Babashoff said. "I don't know why it wasn't obvious to other people, too. I guess I was the scapegoat. Someone had to blame somebody. Something bad had to happen, and it had to happen to me. I didn't get the gold. I got the silver, so I was a loser."

Of course, Babashoff was later proven correct, but the personal toll that she suffered could not be removed. Additionally, the International Olympic Committee has not stripped any of the medals from the East Germans, despite concrete proof.

The only gold medal that Babashoff won at the 1976 Games was from the 400 freestyle relay, where she joined with Kim Peyton, Wendy Boglioli, and Jill Sterkel to defeat the East Germans. That win is considered one of the biggest upsets in Olympic history and was, according to the athletes, the result of the United States' refusal to go home without a gold medal.

"Everyone should be compensated somewhat or just acknowledged," Babashoff said.

Even our own Olympic Committee should step up and have an event where they can invite those who are still alive and recognize them, perhaps with a commemorative medal . . . or at least say, "We know that this has been hard for you." They should at least acknowledge the women. Some people want to think that the issue is over. From our side of it, the whole issue has been shoved under the carpet. I think it is sad. So many women deserved their medals. They were cheated out of their medals at the Olympics. We would like to get what we earned. We were going for the medals, not the cash. We were amateurs. We worked so hard. We earned it and it was stolen right in front of everyone's face and no-one did anything about it. It was like watching a bank robbery where they just let the crooks go and then say, "It's okay."

On the other side, those who were part of the doping program also wonder about what could have been. "The worst thing is they took away from me the opportunity to ever know if I could have won the gold medals without the steroids," Reinisch said. "That's the greatest betrayal of all."

GRAPHS 8.1 AND 8.2

Due to the implementation of a systematic doping program, East Germany dominated women's swimming from 1973 to 1988. Only the fall of the Berlin Wall and the subsequent unveiling of Stasi files revealed the depth of the performance-enhancing drug use. Here is a look at the leading gold medal–winning countries and the leading medal-winning countries in general in major international competition from 1973 to 1988, with the exception of the 1980 and 1984 Olympic Games, which featured boycotts.

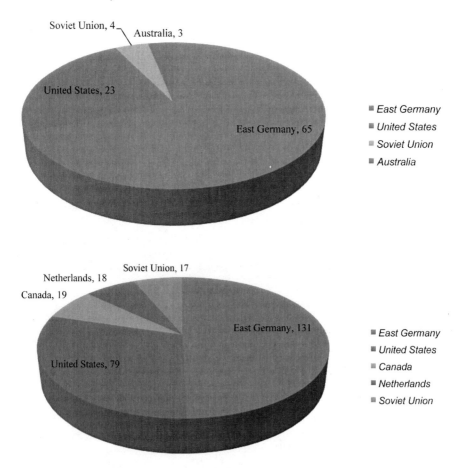

GRAPH 8.3

At the beginning of the 1973 season, the world record in the women's 100 freestyle stood with Australian Shane Gould at 58.50. From 1973 to 1986, the world record in the event was broken on 14 occasions, all by East German athletes later connected to the systematic doping program implemented by their country. It wasn't until 1992 that the record was taken from the grasp of East Germany. Here is a look at how the record progressed.

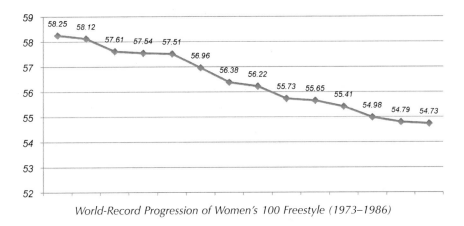

World-Record Progression of Women's 100 Freestyle (1973–1986)

Note: The first 10 world records were established by Kornelia Ender, with Barbara Krause setting the next 3 records. The final world record was set by Kristin Otto, her time of 54.73 enduring until the United States' Jenny Thompson covered the 100 freestyle in 54.48 in 1992.

9

USA All the Way

At the 1976 Olympics in Montreal, the U.S. men put together a performance for the ages, an effort that has never been matched and is unlikely to ever find a peer. The American men won all but one event and shredded the record books in a team showing that was legendary.

Debating the greatest teams in sports history is, more or less, a pointless endeavor. Rarely will a consensus be found. For all those who support the 1927 New York Yankees as the best baseball team of all time, there will be plenty of counterarguments. In the NBA, for every supporter of the 1996 Chicago Bulls as the best of the best, someone will throw support behind the 1986 Boston Celtics or the 1972 Los Angeles Lakers.

If the 1972 Miami Dolphins get the nod as the finest NFL team in history, others will go with the 1985 version of the Chicago Bears or one of Vince Lombardi's esteemed Green Bay Packers squads from the pre–Super Bowl era. Turn to the NHL and you will hear arguments over the candidacy of the 1977 Montreal Canadiens and the 1984 Edmonton Oilers, among other clubs.

For the most part, elite-level swimming is an individual sport, with the team aspect centralized in NCAA competition and major international events, such as the World Championships and Olympic Games. Yet, even though those international meets carry an element of national pride, the bottom line is about which individual got to the wall first.

Despite the sport's primarily individual nature, some teams have stood out through the years but none as prominently as the 1976 U.S. men's Olympic team. The collection of athletes under the watch of legendary coach James "Doc" Counsilman was downright dominant, to the point where it is best to introduce the power of the team in a numerical sense. Consider:

- Of the 13 events contested at the Montreal Games, the United States claimed the gold medal in 12, a winning clip of 92.3 percent. Only the 200 breaststroke proved elusive, with Great Britain's David Wilkie setting a world record as Americans John Hencken and Rick Colella occupied the silver and bronze positions.

- The United States set 11 world records during the championship finals, with Matt Vogel's triumph in the 100 butterfly the only victory that did not arrive in world-record time. Vogel was close, however, falling .08 shy of Mark Spitz's global standard from the 1972 Olympics in Munich.
- At the time of the 1976 Games, each nation was allowed three entries per event, a rule that was reduced to two soon after the United States' overwhelming dominance. With 33 individual medals attainable, the United States claimed 25, a ridiculous podium-finish performance rate of 75.7 percent.
- American athletes swept the podium places in four events: the 200 freestyle, 200 backstroke, 100 butterfly, and 200 butterfly. More, the United States notched gold and silver efforts in five additional events: the 100 freestyle, 400 freestyle, 1500 freestyle, 100 backstroke, and 400 individual medley.
- The United States' two relay wins were blowouts, with the 800 freestyle relay securing a 4-second-plus decision over the Soviet Union and the 400 medley relay beating Canada by more than 3 seconds. Both relays featured John Naber and Jim Montgomery, who emerged as the stars of the Games.

As Montgomery prepared for the 100 freestyle, he was mainly competing against the clock. The heavy favorite to win the gold medal, Montgomery was not likely to finish anywhere lower than on the top step of the medals podium. The real question was whether he could become the first man to break the 50-second barrier.

It had been more than 50 years since Johnny Weissmuller became the first person to complete the 100 freestyle in under a minute, and the long wait for a sub-50-second performance made the event one of the most anticipated of the Games. As Montgomery stormed down the final lap with victory ensured, the spectators kept one eye on him and the other eye on the scoreboard, hoping that it would reveal a never-before-seen figure—and by the smallest margin, it did: Montgomery prevailed in 49.99.

A standing ovation greeted Montgomery as he exited the pool, and Counsilman, who coached Montgomery at Indiana University, made sure that the accomplishment was put in proper context and appreciated to the fullest.

"This will put Montgomery in the Swimming Hall of Fame," Counsilman said. "I think this is the last barrier in swimming. We broke one minute in the 100 freestyle 50 years ago, and I don't think we are going to break 40 seconds. So this is it, at least for a long time. I thought it was the best swim of the Olympics, and we've had some good swims."

If there was one thing missing from Montgomery's shining moment, it was the presence of Jonty Skinner. A South African who trained at the University of Alabama, Skinner, by no fault of his own, was denied the opportunity to duel with Montgomery in Montreal. Due to South Africa's apartheid policies, Skinner's homeland was barred from the biggest sporting event on Earth, a ban not lifted until 1992.

As a result, Montgomery faced a field that was partially diluted. Meanwhile, Skinner was forced to put together a personal Olympics, which came in the form of the Amateur Athletic Union Championships held in Philadelphia 3 weeks after the Olympics. Montgomery, still basking in his Olympic glory, was not present, but Skinner had a target time on his radar and an inkling that Montgomery would be aware of the events that transpired in Philly.

Despite racing against a less-than-Olympic-strong field, Skinner achieved what he set out to accomplish in Philadelphia, blasting Montgomery's newly minted world record with a time of 49.44. Quick math said that the time was more than a half second swifter than Montgomery's "history making" swim and engaged those familiar with the sport in a game of make-believe, as in "What if Montgomery and Skinner were afforded the chance to square off in Montreal? How fast could they have gone?"

"Since I couldn't swim against [Montgomery], my opponent had to be the clock," Skinner said. "I just kept telling myself, 'This is your only chance. Don't blow it.' The Olympics were one day and this was another. I hope Jim was watching me on TV today."

If Montgomery's victory in the 100 freestyle was somewhat lessened by Skinner's exploits a few weeks later, the same cannot be said for what John Naber and Brian Goodell brought to the table. Like Spitz 4 years earlier, Naber was the undisputed star of the American squad, flourishing not only in the water but also as a team leader. A philosophical athlete, Naber routinely saw the big picture and knew how to play the motivation game.

Naber enjoyed the process of becoming a world-record holder, world champion, and Olympic champion, and he wasn't afraid to instill his beliefs in teammates. He also took something more from the team experience than most, probably a reason why Naber was one of the most successful collegiate swimmers in history. While leading the University of Southern California to four NCAA championships during his days as a Trojan, Naber won the 100 and 200 backstrokes in each of his 4 years, along with capturing a pair of 500 freestyle crowns. His 10 individual NCAA titles remain among the most ever by a collegian. It was during this stage of his career in which he developed his cerebral approach to the sport.

"My determination was about 110 percent more than anybody else I've ever known," said Naber, whose confidence and willingness to speak his mind were never questioned. "And for anyone who has the courage to set high goals for themselves, I encourage them to try. But the success in swimming is the journey, not the destination."

As the 1976 Games neared, Naber was expected to carry the banner for the United States. He did not disappoint. He swept the 100 and 200 backstrokes in convincing form, setting world records that endured for 7 years each, proof that Naber was well ahead of his time. While Naber ended the reign of East Germany's Roland Matthes in the 100 backstroke, where Matthes won the bronze medal, Naber's victory in the 200 backstroke was highlighted by the first sub-2-minute effort in history.

For good measure, he won the silver medal in the 200 freestyle, passed in the final meters by fellow American and University of Southern California teammate Bruce

Furniss. There was also a pair of relay triumphs, giving Naber a five-medal haul in his trip north of the border. As much as Naber cherishes the Olympic accomplishments the world got to see, a moment out of the sight of spectators and cameras remains one of his fondest memories from Montreal.

"Long after the award ceremony, [Furniss] and I were still at the pool dressed in street clothes," Naber recalled in a 1988 interview with the *Los Angeles Times*.

> Everybody else was gone. We decided to strip down to our swim suits and do four laps to wind down. After about three and a half easy laps, Bruce said, "Want to race?" I said, "Nah," and then I took off. I got the jump on him and was about to beat him to the wall when he grabbed my trunks. We wrestled in the water for a while, then started laughing. There were no TV cameras, and no one saw this. But it's the moment I think of first when I think of the Olympics.

The 1976 Games figured to be the end of Naber's Olympic days, but the 17-year-old Goodell was expected to have at least two Olympiads to his name. The first went perfectly for an athlete who did not have the typical build of a world-class swimmer. Unlike the 6-foot-6 Naber and other towering figures in the sport, Goodell was 5-foot-8. Nonetheless, he possessed a motor that never yielded and that enabled him to become a distance freestyle great.

While his teammates raked in gold, silver, and bronze medals in Montreal, Goodell left the Olympiad with gold medals in the 400 and 1500 freestyles, each of his victories punctuated by a world record. The standard thought was that Goodell was just hitting the edge of his potential, but Montreal turned out to be the high watermark of his career.

A case of strep throat prevented Goodell from chasing titles at the 1978 World Championships, and political interference robbed him of the opportunity to defend his Olympic titles at the 1980 Games. In Moscow, Goodell was expected to clash with Soviet star Vladimir Salnikov, the eventual champion, in the 400 and 1500 freestyles. But when President Jimmy Carter instituted a U.S. boycott of the Moscow Games, the potential showdowns were erased, along with what Goodell believed would have been the finest hour of his career.

More than three decades later, Goodell still burns over Carter's decision and the impact that it had on the lives of the affected athletes. "I don't like seeing him—in person, on TV, in the newspaper," Goodell said of Carter.

> He's always got something critical to say about somebody else, but when it comes to criticism of the boycott, he can't take it. He's the victim. He can't take being criticized for the most harebrained thing I've ever heard of. I was 17 in Montreal. In Moscow, I would have been 21 and in the prime of my career. And zippo. [Carter] screwed with everybody's lives. I could have made some pretty good coin. It really did screw me up.

For all the success of the American squad, the lone defeat was somewhat of a surprise. As the reigning Olympic champion, John Hencken was widely expected to repeat in the 200 breaststroke, and after his triumph in the 100 breaststroke early in the meet, his prospects only heightened. But Great Britain's David Wilkie had other ideas.

Covering the 200 breaststroke in 2:15.11—a world record that lasted for 6 years—Wilkie left Hencken more than 2 seconds behind and the United States one event shy of a 13-for-13 showing. Given what took place in every other event, it seems ridiculous to spend much time on what did not go right for the United States.

Whether it was Naber winning five medals, the United States sweeping all three medal places in four events, or the Americans claiming 25 pieces of individual hardware, what the Stars and Stripes accomplished in Montreal is hard to fathom. Without question, the United States delivered one of the great team performances in history, regardless of sport.

"The 1976 men's team was special for a variety of reasons," Naber said.

My favorite statistic is that in 13 events, the team was unable to get one gold, one silver and six bronze medals. We so dominated the sport that the next Olympics saw a change in the rules limiting each country to two swimmers per event. I was just one of many swimmers who earned multiple gold medals, and I believe no other team will ever come close to that level of dominance.

GRAPH 9.1

An illustration of the power of the 1976 U.S. men's Olympic team, considered the best in history. While the American squad won 12 of the 13 events on the program, its dominance is even more evident in the number of individual medals collected by team members. Not long after the United States' lopsided showing, which included a sweep of the podium in four events, a rule change was implemented that dropped the number of entries per country from three to two.

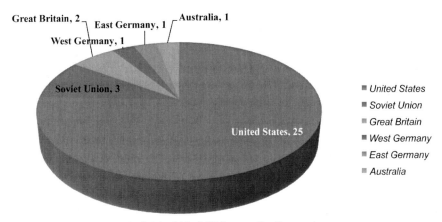

Individual Medal Winners (By Country)

10

Brigitha Breaks Barrier

In 1976, Dutchwoman Enith Brigitha made history when she became the first black swimmer to medal at the Olympic Games, earning bronze medals in the 100 and 200 freestyles. Like many others, though, Brigitha was a victim of East Germany's systematic doping program, which robbed her of greater Olympic glory.

Barrier-breaking moments hold special moments in sporting lore, from the day that Jackie Robinson became the first African American to play in Major League Baseball to Tiger Woods becoming the first black golfer to win a major championship, accomplishing that feat in grand fashion and on a lily-white stage at the 1997 Masters.

The history of swimming, like golf, has been largely devoid of black athletes. Scan the starting blocks of most major meets through the years, and athletes of color are truly the exception. In recent years, the United States has had better representation on its international squads, most notably Olympic medalist sprinters Cullen Jones and Anthony Ervin.

For his part, Jones has taken a prominent role in encouraging African American youngsters to get involved in swimming but not because he is concerned with churning out Olympic champions. Rather, Jones is well aware of the fact that drowning deaths among African American children are significantly higher than the figures of white children. Jones has firsthand experience in this area, having nearly drowned as a child.

Given the low percentage of black involvement in swimming, what Enith Brigitha pulled off in the 1970s is an astounding accomplishment. The sad part is that Brigitha, who represented the Netherlands, has not received the attention that she deserves. After all, she is a barrier-breaking performer who set a standard for her race.

Born in the island nation of Curacao, part of the Kingdom of the Netherlands, Brigitha became a rare swimming star from her region of the world. By the time that she was 17 years old, Brigitha had qualified to compete for the Netherlands at the 1972 Games in Munich. Although she failed to medal in her first Olympic appearance, she provided plenty of reason to believe that the future was bright.

In addition to placing sixth in the 100 and 200 backstrokes, Brigitha advanced to the final of the 100 freestyle, where she finished eighth. The success that she exhibited was just a precursor of what was to come. The next year, at the inaugural World Championships, Brigitha stood on the podium with a silver medal from the 200 backstroke and a bronze medal from the 100 freestyle.

Brigitha's momentum continued a year later when she won five medals—two silver, three bronze—at the European Championships, and it was maintained at the 1975 World Championships, where Brigitha was the bronze medalist in the 100 and 200 freestyles. These various performances set the stage for her second Olympiad.

Although no longer an unknown commodity on the international scene, Brigitha did not receive the proper credit that she deserved at the 1976 Games. In Montreal, the Dutchwoman won bronze medals in the 100 and 200 freestyles, in the process becoming the first black swimmer to medal at the Olympic Games. On their own merit, the accomplishments are impressive, but they could and should have been greater had Brigitha—like others at the time—not been victimized by the systematic doping program that vaulted East German athletes to countless titles during the 1970s and 1980s.

As documents from the Stasi, the East German secret police, were revealed after the fall of the Berlin Wall in 1989, years of suspicion concerning performance-enhancing drug use by East German athletes morphed into concrete evidence. The documents proved that East Germany's coaches had placed its athletes on regimented drug programs designed to bolster their performances.

For Brigitha, the use of performance-enhancing drugs by her East German rivals cost the Dutch star her proper place in history. Today, Suriname's Anthony Nesty is known as the first black swimmer to win Olympic gold, having prevailed in the 100 butterfly at the 1988 Games in Seoul. Brigitha, though, could have held that distinction 12 years earlier. In the 100 freestyle, Brigitha was beaten to the wall by only Kornelia Ender and Petra Priemer, East Germans who were among those given steroids by their coaches.

Through the years, there have been several calls and appeals for Olympic medals to be redistributed from Olympiads tainted by East German doping. But the International Olympic Committee has opted to ignore the issue, despite the fact that it has stripped medals from other athletes implicated with doping, such as American track star Marion Jones.

"Every once in a while, we've looked at the issue hypothetically," stated Canadian Dick Pound, a 1960 Olympic swimmer and former vice president of the International Olympic Committee. "But it's just a nightmare when you try to rejigger what you think might have been history. For the IOC to step in and make these God-like decisions as to who should have gotten what . . . it's just a bottomless swamp."

With the considerable number of doping violations that have revealed themselves over time, Pound's words contain a measure of truth. Indeed, it would be a difficult task to determine how to reissue medals to those affected by their rivals' doping violations. But to simply take a shrug-of-the-shoulders approach is insulting to athletes such as Brigitha and the United States' Shirley Babashoff, whose willingness to speak out against the East Germans was met with harsh criticism.

Whenever the subject of East German doping arises, Babashoff's name is immediately mentioned. On three occasions at the 1976 Olympics, Babashoff won a silver medal behind an East German in an individual event. Brigitha, though, ranks right with Babashoff when it comes to being victimized.

Of the 11 individual medals that Brigitha won among the Olympic Games, World Championships, and European Championships, 10 events featured the Dutchwoman finishing behind at least one East German. Had doping not been a foe, it is a certainty that Brigitha would be a member of the International Swimming Hall of Fame. Truthfully, she is deserving of that honor even without a gold medal in major international competition, such was her consistency.

In many of her silver and bronze medal showings, including both her Olympic events from 1976, Brigitha placed behind Ender. The East German is one of several athletes from her era to admit to the systematic doping program. In a different way, Ender was a victim among others, a pawn in a political system obsessed with sporting success.

"Now, after all this time, I still ask myself whether it could be possible they gave me things because I remember being given injections during training and competition, but this was explained to me as being substances to help me regenerate and recuperate," Ender said.

It was natural to think this way because the distance swimmers had more injections than we did as sprinters. It's very sad. The only losers in that are the athletes.

It is easy for [the East German coaches and doctors] to state these things now. The finger of blame is pointed at us, not them, and we knew nothing of these things they did. They deserve [punishment]. The medical men are the real guilty people. They know what they have done. When they gave us things to help us "regenerate," we were never asked if we wanted it. It was just given.

Named the Dutch Sportswoman of the Year on two occasions, Brigitha totaled 21 Dutch titles during her career and 14 major international medals, including relay events. On a personal level, she considers herself an Olympic champion, regardless of what the official record books state.

"It's hard to stomach that, despite the evidence, admissions and documentation of systematic steroid use of the East Germans, no Olympic medals have been reissued," wrote Mike Gustafson in a piece that he penned for USA Swimming.

While so many swimmers have given up hope, there is still an urgency and a fight to pursue the reissuing of these medals.

To date, no East German medals have been stripped after the widespread doping surfaced, and record books don't list Enith Brigitha as the first-ever black Olympic gold medalist. Like a tarnished record, her gold remains a darkened bronze.

11

Political Pawns

The powerhouse American program was missing from the 1980 Games in Moscow, due to the boycott instituted by President Jimmy Carter in response to the Soviet Union's invasion of Afghanistan. The decision denied many athletes the opportunity to chase their Olympic dreams.

It has long been stated, to the point of cliché, that sports and politics do not mix. Generally speaking, fans prefer their sports for what they are: athletic entertainment. They want to see their team score the most points and ultimately hoist a championship trophy. They are not interested in an athlete's refusal to stand for the national anthem. They do not want to hear an athlete's support or criticism of the president's stance on a major issue.

Certainly, fans do not want to see athletes caught in political crossfire, exactly what transpired more than 30 years ago when U.S. president Jimmy Carter basically threw aspiring Olympians on a land mine. The decision seemed faulty at the time and now remains flawed, with the benefit of historical perspective.

Thousands of training hours were wasted. Hundreds of miles in the water—all that solitary time in the pool—went for naught. Dreams were crushed. It was a painful time, to say the least, and not just for the swimmers. The boycott was a brutal reality, too, for track athletes, wrestlers, boxers, rowers, and competitors in the other Olympic sports.

When the Soviet Union invaded Afghanistan in 1979, opposition to the movement was vocal, and Cold War tensions heightened between the Soviet Union and the United States. Still, there wasn't any immediate thought that the invasion would affect the biggest sporting event in the world. That thought process changed, however, in January 1980 when President Carter went public with a plan to boycott the 1980 Olympic Games in Moscow.

On January 20, Carter went on the television program *Meet the Press* and officially threatened a U.S. boycott of the 22nd Olympiad. While the threat was concerning to the athletes possessing Olympic hopes, it was still far from a lock. In his speech, Carter spoke of his personal preference for a boycott, at the same time including the American people's beliefs, even if they were unclear.

"Neither I nor the American people would favor the sending of an American team to Moscow with Soviet invasion troops in Afghanistan," Carter said.

I've sent a message today to the United States Olympic Committee spelling out my own position that unless the Soviets withdraw their troops, within a month, from Afghanistan, that the Olympic Games be moved from Moscow to an alternate site, or multiple sites, or postponed, or canceled. If the Soviets do not withdraw their troops from Afghanistan, within a month, I would not support the sending of an American team to the Olympics.

It's very important for the world to realize how serious a threat the Soviet's invasion of Afghanistan is. I do not want to inject politics into the Olympics, and I would personally favor the establishment of a permanent Olympic site for both the summer and the winter games. In my opinion, the most appropriate permanent site for the summer games would be Greece. This will be my own position, and I have asked the U.S. Olympics Committee to take this position to the International Olympics Committee and I would hope that as many nations as possible would support this basic position. One hundred and four nations voted against the Soviet invasion and called for their immediate withdraw from Afghanistan, in the United Nations, and I would hope that as many of those as possible would support the position I've just outlined to you.

Although Carter indicated that he did not want to inject politics into sports, that position is exactly the scenario he favored. Following the announcement of his intentions, Carter successfully convinced U.S. politicians and the U.S. Olympic Committee that his plan was the correct course of action.

On March 21, 1980, Carter made the U.S. boycott of the Moscow Games official when he met with approximately 100 Olympic hopefuls and outlined the reasons for his decision. The speech was filled with remorse for the athletes' loss of their dreams. At the time, reaction was mixed. Some athletes were disappointed. Some were angry. Some, who did not want to go against the decision of the national leader, expressed understanding.

"It is absolutely imperative that we and other nations who believe in freedom and who believe in human rights and who believe in peace let our voices be heard in an absolutely clear way, and not add the imprimatur of approval to the Soviet Union and its government while they have 105,000 heavily armed invading forces in the freedom-loving and innocent and deeply religious country of Afghanistan," Carter said.

Thousands of people's lives have already been lost. Entire villages have been wiped out deliberately by the Soviet invading forces. And as you well know, the people in the Soviet Union don't even know it. They do not even realize that 104 nations in the United Nations condemned the Soviet Union for their invasion and called for their immediate withdrawal from Afghanistan. The people of the Soviet Union don't even know it.

The Olympics are important to the Soviet Union. They have made massive investments in buildings, equipment, propaganda. As has probably already been pointed out to you, they have passed out hundreds of thousands of copies of an official Soviet document saying that the decision of the world community to hold the Olympics in Moscow is an acknowledgement of approval of the foreign policy of the Soviet Union, and proof to the world that the Soviets' policy results in international peace.

I can't say at this moment what other nations will not go to the Summer Olympics in Moscow. Ours will not go. I say that not with any equivocation. The decision has been made. The American people are convinced that we should not go to the Summer Olympics. The Congress has voted overwhelmingly, almost unanimously, which is a very rare thing, that we will not go. And I can tell you that many of our major allies, particularly those democratic countries who believe in freedom, will not go.

I understand how you feel, and I thought about it a lot as we approached this moment, when I would have to stand here in front of fine young Americans and dedicated coaches, who have labored sometimes for more than 10 years, in every instance for years, to become among the finest athletes in the world, knowing what the Olympics mean to you, to know that you would be disappointed. It's not a pleasant time for me.

You occupy a special place in American life, not because of your talent or your dedication or your training or your commitment or your ability as an athlete, but because for American people, Olympic athletes represent something else. You represent the personification of the highest ideals of our country. You represent a special commitment to the value of a human life, and to the achievement of excellence within an environment of freedom, and a belief in truth and friendship and respect for others, and the elimination of discrimination, and the honoring of human rights, and peace.

Even though many of you may not warrant or deserve that kind of esteem, because you haven't thought so deeply about these subjects, perhaps, the American people think you do, because you are characterized accurately as clean and decent and honest and dedicated.

In his speech, Carter claimed that he knew how the athletes felt about his decision, citing the amount of time that they dedicated to their craft and the pursuit of excellence in a specific endeavor. Yet, how could Carter have actually known? He wasn't an athlete waking before sunrise and training for countless hours. He wasn't an athlete postponing the next phase in life to chase a dream, one that offers itself to a miniscule percentage of individuals. Carter might have understood that there was hurt, but to state that he knew how that pain felt was an insult to the athletes. Not surprisingly, many athletes harbored ill will toward Carter, disgust that remains to this day.

Ultimately, Carter convinced numerous nations to follow the United States' lead and take part in the boycott. More than 60 nations boycotted the Moscow Games, their athletes realizing the same fate as American hopefuls.

In the case of Brian Goodell, the 1980 Games were supposed to be a legacy-building opportunity. Four years earlier, Goodell was a member of the legendary U.S. men's team that won 12 of the 13 swimming events in Montreal. Goodell was the gold medalist in the 400 and 1500 freestyles, and defense of his crowns in 1980 was well within reach, especially considering that Goodell was 21 and flourishing.

Although Soviet Vladimir Salnikov had emerged as a major threat in the distance events, Goodell was confident that he could retain his crowns. But because of Carter's decision, we will never know. More, the aquatic world was deprived of a pair of showdowns between Goodell and Salnikov, who went on to win gold medals in the 400 and 1500 freestyles.

"I was 17 in Montreal," Goodell said.

In Moscow, I would have been 21 and in the prime of my career. And zippo. [Carter] screwed with everybody's lives. I could have made some pretty good coin. It really did screw me up. It totally derailed me and changed my life. I didn't know what to do with myself. My life took a totally different path than what I had expected. I was pretty clearly depressed. I couldn't get up in the morning. Never got help, but I should have. I've tried to forget it a zillion times, but I'm still disgusted.

More than 30 years later, Goodell's anger toward Carter has not subsided. He, like many others, cannot wrap his mind around the decision that was made. His career ended not in fine fashion but with a political whimper that was out of his control. The mere sight or mention of Carter's name riles Goodell.

"I don't like seeing him. In person. On TV. In the newspaper," Goodell said. "He's always got something critical to say about somebody else but when it comes to criticism of the boycott, he can't take it. He's the victim. He can't take being criticized for the most hair-brained thing I've ever heard of. I never got a chance to prove how good I was."

While the boycott spelled the end of Goodell's career, it robbed Cynthia Woodhead of her best chance at Olympic gold. At the time of the 1980 Olympics, Woodhead was the world-record holder in the 200 freestyle and, along with Mary T. Meagher and Tracy Caulkins, among the few athletes capable of defeating the steroid-boosted East German women.

Woodhead could have contended for five medals at the 1980 Games, exactly the medal haul that she managed at the 1978 World Championships. Instead, the 16-year-old was forced to wonder what could have been and to battle her emotions.

"I was very depressed and disillusioned by the whole thing," Woodhead said. "It was tough enough being a teenager, plus this. And there was nobody to relate to. So I used to just walk out of school and leave. Somehow, my parents, my teachers, everyone dealt with it. They knew that I didn't want anyone to see me cry."

Illness and injury hampered Woodhead in the 2 years after the Moscow boycott, but she rallied to win the 200 freestyle at the 1983 Pan American Games, where she also won the silver medal in the 400 freestyle. In 1984, Woodhead got her Olympic wish when she qualified for the Los Angeles Games. However, she was not in the form that she knew several years earlier.

At those 1984 Games, Woodhead valiantly battled in her prime event, the 200 freestyle, but ended up with the silver medal, finishing behind teammate Mary Wayte. Woodhead was also more than a second slower than her personal best, proof that her best chance to win Olympic gold was lost to politics.

"It was awful," Woodhead said. "Those four years [between Moscow and Los Angeles] felt like 10. It seemed like everything went wrong. But I felt I owed it to myself to compete in 1984, make the team, and actually go to an Olympics, so I pressed on. I enjoyed it, but I didn't. It felt like I was watching a movie and wishing I could have been there in my top form, at my peak. It certainly wasn't a highlight of my life."

The same frustration did not beset Woodhead's American teammates Rowdy Gaines, Meagher, and Caulkins. Like Woodhead, all three were caught up in the 1980 boycott and at the peak of their careers. Yet, they were able to win Olympic gold at the Los Angeles Games. The pain of 1980 could never be entirely erased, but their success in 1984 at least eased the sting.

Considered the most versatile woman in American swimming history, Caulkins won the 200 and 400 individual medleys in Los Angeles, in addition to helping the U.S. 400 medley relay to victory. But when she digests her Olympic experiences, she cannot fully separate herself from Carter's decision.

"What really hits home to me about the boycott was the Soviets didn't pull out of Afghanistan for nine years," Caulkins said. "Did it put any pressure on them? No. It was just a missed opportunity for many athletes. It just doesn't seem fair."

Meagher was so far ahead of her time in the 100 and 200 butterflies that her world records endured for almost two decades. Of any of the athletes affected by the 1980 boycott, it would be difficult to find anyone considered more of a lock to win than the woman dubbed "Madame Butterfly." Meagher had established such a gap between herself and the rest of the world that the 1980 Games figured to be her coronation.

Fortunately for Meagher, she continued to pursue her dream and was able to win the 100 and 200 butterflies in 1984, along with a relay gold. But like Caulkins, there were difficult moments throughout her journey, especially from a mental perspective.

"I don't want this to get out of proportion, but when I hit rock bottom, one of the things that came to mind was suicide," Meagher said. "I mean, what an easy way out. The counselor said to me, 'You'll never be creative enough to figure out how to be happy with the circumstances in your life now if in the back of your mind, you're always thinking there's an easy way out.'"

Gaines—who has remained in the sport as a commentator—temporarily retired between Moscow and Los Angeles, only to find the lure of the Olympics pulling him back. Racing the blue-ribbon event, the 100 freestyle, Gaines won his elusive gold and supported the effort with a pair of relay triumphs.

"I felt physically at my peak in 1980—and mentally up, too," Gaines said.

It was tough, really tough. I had a chance for four golds. It was a long four years. There were a lot of peaks and valleys. I almost quit a few times. In fact, I actually did retire for six months in 1981 just after I finished college, but I couldn't stay away. I felt something was missing in my life. I looked back and realized it was the Olympics. Just to get a chance to compete. It was tugging at me.

But what about those athletes who never got their chance at Olympic glory? Some opted to end their careers after the 1980 boycott, citing the need to move on in life.

Others could not get past the pain of the boycott, their devastated emotions driving them away from the sport. Still, others continued to pursue their Olympic dream, only to come up short in their attempt.

Craig Beardsley knows the feeling of being robbed. Before President Carter announced the U.S. boycott of the Moscow Games, Beardsley was considered the favorite to win the gold medal in the 200 butterfly. Not only was he the reigning Pan American champion in the event, but his best times were also going to be difficult for anyone to match.

So, when the boycott became official, Beardsley was certainly an athlete who felt shafted. Indeed, he likely would have won gold at the 1980 Games. A week after the Soviet Union's Sergey Fesenko won the Olympic gold medal in the 200 butterfly with a time of 1:59.76, Beardsley obliterated that mark when he raced to a world record of 1:58.21 in Irvine, California.

"People forget what happened in 1980," Beardsley said.

> You meet people, and once they find out you were a swimmer, they usually ask, "Did you go to the Olympics?" It's never an easy answer, and there's always a footnote. When they ask, "Oh, did you get a medal?" it's kind of hard to tell them that I was not there because then you have to go into the whole story, and the last thing I'm looking for is sympathy. I just try to avoid the question and change the subject.

Rather than retire after the 1980 Olympics, Beardsley continued with his career. He set another world record in 1981 and repeated as the Pan American champion in the 200 butterfly in 1983, along with winning the bronze medal in his prime event at the 1982 World Championships. But when the 1984 U.S. Olympic Trials rolled around, fate was not on Beardsley's side.

As Pablo Morales and Patrick Kennedy finished first and second in the 200 butterfly at Trials, Beardsley was the odd man out as the third-place finisher. Making matters more difficult to digest, the year 1984 marked the first time in which countries were limited to two swimmers in each event, as opposed to the three entries that formerly was the standard.

"I was devastated," said Beardsley, who did not watch any of the 1984 Games on television. "I felt I owed it to so many people who had stuck with me.

> [In 1980], I don't want to say that I supported the boycott, but I wasn't against it, either. I tried to think there was some good in it. We were doing the right thing. I supported everything at that time. However, I began to realize that it was just another political movement. I became strongly opinionated about trying to separate sports and politics. It will never happen again. Sports, like music, is one of those great things that bind people together.

For every 1980 athlete affected by the boycott, there was a 1984 athlete who watched hard work get washed away. In retaliation for the American-led boycott, the Eastern Bloc nations turned their backs on the 1984 Games, a gesture that seemed to say, "We can play that game, too." Of course, the athletes—again—were the victims, with the Soviet Union's Vladimir Salnikov among the leading losers.

Regarded as one of the premier distance freestylers in history, Salnikov won Olympic gold in 1980 in the 400 and 1500 freestyles, events that he also won at the World Championships in 1978 and 1982. Had the Soviet Union not boycotted the Los Angeles Olympiad, Salnikov likely would have defended his titles. After all, he posted times during that summer that eclipsed the winning marks of the Olympic Games.

Missing the Los Angeles Games figured to mark the end of Salnikov's Olympic excellence, but the Soviet pushed forward in the years leading to the 1988 Olympics in Seoul. Although he was not the unbeatable force that the globe knew in the first half of the 1980s, he was nonetheless a factor. And when he went to Seoul and retained his Olympic crown in the 1500 freestyle, it was a major statement.

Just before midnight on the night that he regained Olympic glory, Salnikov wandered into the dining hall at the athletes' village and received his proper due. Around 300 fellow Olympians temporarily dropped their forks and knives and paid homage to the "Monster of the Waves" with a standing ovation befitting an Olympic icon.

"[Political leaders] used us as pawns in their game," Salnikov said of the boycott that deprived him.

I was shocked when I heard about the boycott. I felt emptiness inside me. My first desire was to quit, but after I thought about it, I realized that would only make me feel even worse. And I kept training more intensely than ever before so I could not think of anything else.

If I had won in Los Angeles, I probably would have retired soon thereafter. But I stayed in the sport and won in 1988 when almost everyone had given up on me.

Simply, the boycott was a no-win situation for anyone involved. For Carter, whose one-term presidency was viewed as one of the weakest in history, the boycott is a black mark of his career. It accomplished nothing. Meanwhile, hardworking athletes across all sports were robbed of their dreams. Some were fortunate enough to earn a chance at Olympic glory 4 years later. Others were not so fortunate.

Nonetheless, all the athletes affected by the 1980 boycott share a similar question pertaining to the Moscow Games: What could have been?

12

Rowdy's Reaction

At the height of his career, Rowdy Gaines was denied the opportunity to find Olympic glory, with the U.S. boycott of the 1980 Games in Moscow keeping Gaines at home. But 4 years later, Gaines atoned for his missed chance, with some critical coaching advice playing a major role in his success.

Through history, sports and politics have frequently run along parallel lines, their paths eventually colliding with ugly results. There has been no bigger stage for these clashes than the Olympic Games, the quadrennial event that brings together countries with differing governments, cultures, socioeconomic statuses, and religious beliefs.

At the 1936 Olympics in Berlin, Adolf Hitler used Germany's role as host to promote the Nazi party and its ideals and to emphasize his perceived superiority of the Aryan race. While Hitler had a global forum, his plan was significantly hindered by American Jesse Owens. As Hitler looked on, the African American track star short-circuited any suggestions of Aryan supremacy by winning four gold medals in dominant fashion.

Thirty-two years later, the United States' Tommie Smith and John Carlos ran to gold and bronze medals, respectively, in the 200-meter dash at the 1968 Olympics in Mexico City. But it is their actions during the medal ceremony, not their speed, that are remembered most. In protest of civil rights inequality for African Americans, Smith and Carlos each bowed their heads and raised a black-gloved fist into the air, a known symbol for black power, during the playing of the "Star Spangled Banner." They also stood in black socks and no shoes, meant to represent black poverty.

The actions of Smith and Carlos were deemed inappropriate by many, including the International Olympic Committee. Under pressure from the committee, the U.S. Olympic Committee suspended the athletes, who were subsequently thrown out of the Olympic Village. To this day, the picture of Smith and Carlos on the podium is an iconic image in Olympic history. Olympic history, too, knows Rowdy Gaines—and Gaines knows the combustible relationship between athletics and politics.

As the 1980 Games in Moscow neared, Gaines was expected to be one of the American stars of the 22nd Olympiad, along with countrywomen Tracy Caulkins and Mary T. Meagher. As a star for Auburn University, Gaines was surging at the right time, his peak performances seemingly destined for the summer of 1980. If the blueprint unfolded according to plan, Gaines would be a gold medal favorite in the 100 and 200 freestyles and as a member of two U.S. relays.

While Gaines was training for the biggest moment of his career, the Soviet Union invaded Afghanistan in December 1979 in support of the Afghan communist government's conflict with anticommunist Muslim guerillas. A month later, U.S. president Jimmy Carter gave a speech that described several reactionary measures to the Soviet Union's invasion of Afghanistan. One measure was a boycott of the Moscow Games if Soviet troops did not withdraw.

"Although the United States would prefer not to withdraw from the Olympic games scheduled in Moscow this summer, the Soviet Union must realize that its continued aggressive actions will endanger both the participation of athletes and the travel to Moscow by spectators who would normally wish to attend the Olympic games," Carter said in his speech.

On March 21, 1980, the hammer dropped. Meeting with 150 American athletes, Carter announced that the United States would officially boycott the Olympic Games. With that one decision, which was mimicked by 60 other countries, hundreds of American athletes saw their Olympic dreams crushed. Years of hard work, dedication, and sacrifice went to waste. Gaines was one of the athletes who was robbed.

"I never believed for a moment that we would actually boycott," Gaines said.

In fact, I was in denial all the way until they made the official announcement. . . . I think the boycott was made for two reasons. One was to influence the [Soviets] to leave Afghanistan. The other was to try and move the Olympics out of [the Soviet Union]. Neither one worked. If it truly would have helped the cause, then I would have been for it as well. But the old cliché of mixing politics and sports is so true. The [Soviets] used it to their advantage by winning more medals and the propaganda helped them tremendously and it ruined so many people's athletic careers. The best thing we could do then was to go over there and kick their ass.

Like many athletes of the era, Gaines faced decisions in the aftermath of the boycott. Following his senior year at Auburn, Gaines had to decide whether to continue with the sport and pursue a berth to the 1984 Olympics in Los Angeles or retire. It was not an easy decision considering what Gaines had accomplished in the preceding months. Simply, he was on the finest roll of his career.

In addition to setting a world record in the 200 freestyle ahead of the 1980 Olympics, Gaines set a world record in the 100 freestyle in 1981. But for a 6-month period after his senior year of college, Gaines could not see sticking with the pool through 1984. At the time, the end of a collegiate career typically coincided with retirement, due to the truly amateur status of the sport. For Gaines, it was time to walk away . . . at least temporarily.

"It was a very difficult decision," Gaines said.

In fact, I retired after my senior year in 1981 because that's what you did back then. There was no swimming after you graduated from college because there was no money. I wasn't even allowed to accept money. It was still truly an amateur sport back then. After being retired for those six months, my father came to me and said that I would have a hard time the rest of my life looking in the mirror and saying "what if" and he was right, I didn't want to have that feeling. It was not easy though. I worked as a night clerk in a hotel to try and make some money to survive, lived in a hovel and survived on mac and cheese. But there were a lot of us doing that so there was camaraderie with those that were boycott babies.

Gaines's comeback from his brief retirement got off to a positive start, with Gaines breaking his world record in the 200 freestyle at the U.S. World Championships Trials in July 1982. He followed by winning silver medals at the World Champs in the 100 and 200 freestyles and anchored three gold medal–winning relays.

But the next summer did not produce the results that Gaines was chasing at the Pan American Games. While he won the 100 freestyle and was the bronze medalist in the 200 freestyle, the performances lacked the pop that was a familiar trademark. With the Olympic Games and redemption a year away, Gaines hardly put fear into his rivals. Questions began to creep into Gaines's mind.

"I sort of felt [doubt] in the summer of 1983 after the Pan Am Games," he said.

I swam really poorly there. It was the first time in such a meet that I didn't improve my times. I didn't even win the 200, the event in which I held the world record. I won the 100 and was on three winning relay teams, which sounds OK, but I knew the competition wasn't that strong, not like it would be in the Olympics. For the first time, I felt old. I had doubts. I sat down with my parents, my coaches and my friends, all of whom really helped me. And in the end, I decided to go for it—win, lose or draw—because otherwise I would never know.

The 1984 Olympic Trials did not exactly boost Gaines's confidence, either. He didn't even qualify for the Los Angeles Games in the 200 freestyle—individually or as a relay member—and he was only second to Mike Heath in the 100 freestyle, although that placement officially secured his Olympic invitation. Could Gaines get it together in time to excel in the biggest meet of his life? It was a legitimate concern.

The 100 freestyle was the first event of Gaines's Olympic program, and he was racing in a stacked field. Although the Eastern Bloc countries boycotted the Games in retaliation for what took place in 1980, Gaines had to deal with formidable competition in Heath, Australia's Mark Stockwell, and Sweden's Per Johansson. A medal of any color was far from a guarantee, let alone a gold medal.

As Gaines was preparing for the final, he was approached by his coach, Richard Quick, and told to prepare for a quick start by the referee, Francisco Silvestri of Panama. One of the greatest coaches in the world, Quick was attentive to details. From what he witnessed at the 1982 World Championships and 1983 Pan American

Games, Quick knew that Silvestri had a quick trigger when starting races, and he wanted Gaines to be alert for a similar outcome.

Indeed, Quick's advice paid dividends. After the finalists in the 100 freestyle climbed the starting blocks, Silvestri's reputation played out. As many of the swimmers were still moving downward to the "set" position, Silvestri fired his starter's pistol. Ready for the quick fire, Gaines surged off the blocks and immediately bolted to a half-body-length lead. Meanwhile, Stockwell was left behind, with Heath even farther back.

Gaines made the turn at the halfway mark in front of the pack, aware of his lead. As he made his way down the last lap, he kept reminding himself to dig deep and push as hard as he could in what would be the last individual race of his career. Although Stockwell was closing during the final strokes, Gaines got to the wall first in 49.80, with Stockwell earning the silver medal in 50.24. Johansson placed third in 50.31, just ahead of Heath in 50.41.

After turning to read the scoreboard, a jubilant Gaines threw his head back and jumped into the air, thrusting his right arm upward. Four years after what should have been his handshake with Olympic glory, Gaines recognized his career dream.

"Part of me feels like it was yesterday," Gaines said. "I can remember specific details of the race. But another part me feels like that was another person. I'm not sure how I did all that. It would have been impossible without Richard Quick. He had such a knack for picking up things to help his athletes, and that's what he did with the start. But more than a coach, he was always a confidant and friend."

The excitement of Gaines was equally matched by the anger of Stockwell and Heath. The Australian, knowing that he wasn't set for the start of the race, twice slammed his fist against the wall but then congratulated Gaines. The Australian delegation filed a protest on Stockwell's behalf, but it was denied. As for Heath, he congratulated Gaines before exiting the pool irate with the start and the way that it cost him early ground.

"I don't want to take away anything from Rowdy," Stockwell said. "I mean, he's great. He's been around for a long time and he knows what to look out for. It just wasn't a fair start."

Gaines might have been forced to wait for his Olympic experience, but he certainly got the most out of the occasion. After winning the 100 freestyle, Gaines powered the United States to gold medals in the 400 freestyle relay and 400 medley relay, giving him three victories on his home soil. However, it would not be the last of his Olympic dalliances.

Following his athletic career, Gaines became involved in broadcasting and has been a commentator at every Olympic Games since 1992. The 2016 Olympics in Rio de Janeiro will be his seventh Olympiad behind the microphone. Listening to a broadcast in which Gaines is involved leaves no doubt about his genuine care for what is taking place in the pool. He is highly excitable, his voice frequently rising to a crescendo as a down-to-the-wire race is decided at the wall.

Although some fans of the sport object to Gaines's approach, he doesn't apologize for his style. Enthusiasm is his calling card. Perhaps his most famous call was at the 2008 Olympics in Beijing, when Jason Lezak anchored the United States to an improbable victory in the 400 freestyle relay, in the process keeping alive Michael Phelps's pursuit of eight gold medals.

"The first and foremost thing I try to bring to my announcing is passion," Gaines said. "People can question some of my knowledge and my language or grammar, but they can't question my passion. I hope that's something that comes across because it's genuine and I love doing it. I have the best seat in the house."

An affable man who remains active in operating swim clinics, Gaines is one of the most recognizable faces of the sport. He can tell stories about races that he has witnessed and ones in which he has taken part. It would be difficult to find a better story than the tale of his 1984 gold medal, which capped a journey from heartache to elation.

"I'll tell you the truth. I was preparing my loser's speech," Gaines said of 1984.

I felt if I lost, I would come out and be gracious. I was going to say that I thought I had contributed to the sport and that I've got nothing to be ashamed of. It would hurt for the rest of my life. But I would have said it was worth it.

[Olympic coach Don Gambril] realized that I needed to stick around for my own sense of sanity. I think if I had quit, 20 years down the line I would have jumped out of the 20th floor, just from wondering if I could have made it or not. I felt in my heart that I needed to do this. He asked me if it was worth it. I told him, yeah, it was worth it. I'd go through another 4 years for this feeling. There's so many of us who have been around for so long [since the 1980 boycott]. You might get tired of hearing it, but we went through hell in 1980. But it was worth it.

13

A Tie Game

At the 1984 Olympics in Los Angeles, American teammates Carrie Steinseifer and Nancy Hogshead touched the wall, looked to the scoreboard, and smiled at one another. They had tied for the gold medal in the 100 freestyle, marking the first shared gold medal in the sport's Olympic history.

Scoreboards at the biggest events are filled with all sorts of key information. Name, country, lane assignment, time, and place are the most common pieces of info, with other details typically available, too, such as split times and the world record. But any athlete with international experience will indicate which column is the most important.

While developing swimmers are primarily occupied with improving their times from meet to meet, veterans are more concerned with where they finish. Sure, they want to post their fastest performances, as a top finish typically requires such an outing. But the common refrain among the elite goes something like this: "I just wanted to get my hand on the wall first. That's all that mattered."

That refrain explains why the top-tier athletes in events such as the Olympics have similar reactions at the conclusion of their races. They will touch the wall, then with a quick jerk turn to the scoreboard, their eyes darting to the placement column. Time is secondary. All they want to know is the finishing order and whether a trip to the medals podium is in their future.

At the 1984 Olympics in Los Angeles, the scoreboard initially brought confusion to the finish of the women's 100 freestyle, only to reveal the first official tie in Olympic swimming history, a shared gold medal by American teammates Nancy Hogshead, a veteran, and Carrie Steinseifer, an up-and-coming teenager. How the women came to experience the Olympics is a tale of two glories, one gut-wrenching road and the other a more traditional route.

By the time that Hogshead was a 12-year-old, she was tabbed for stardom. A multievent talent who flourished in the freestyle and butterfly events, an Olympic future figured to be on the horizon. Not only was Hogshead a nationally ranked swimmer, but she vaulted to No. 1 in the world in the 200 butterfly. Eyes were on her, including those of her American teammates. They knew that the young upstart was an obstacle in the pursuit of their success, and resentment occasionally filled the air.

But Hogshead shook off the jealousy and continued to pursue her goals. At the 1978 World Championships in Berlin, she won the silver medal in the 200 butterfly and appeared on her way to claiming some hardware at the 1980 Olympics in Moscow. Of course, that blueprint never panned out, due to President Jimmy Carter imposing a U.S. boycott of the Games, a political move that was a response to the Soviet Union's invasion of Afghanistan.

"I remember watching the 1976 Olympics," Hogshead once said. "I was completely taken, not just with swimming, but with track and field and gymnastics and basketball and volleyball. I loved the whole thing, this idea that this was the best in the world competing against each other. It sung to me."

Because the Olympics tugged so heartily at Hogshead, she chose to continue her swimming career after 1980 while many of her teammates from that Olympic squad opted for retirement. She eventually enrolled at Duke University and began the road toward the 1984 Olympics in Los Angeles. But on that path, Hogshead endured one of the most emotionally devastating events a woman can experience: she was raped.

During a November 1981 training run near the Duke campus, Hogshead sensed something was amiss as she encountered a slow-running man moving in her direction. Indeed, Hogshead's intuitions were correct, as the stranger grabbed her and pulled her into a tree-lined area. Well muscled and conditioned from her aquatic background, Hogshead was able to fend off the man for approximately 30 minutes before she lost the fight and was raped.

"I actually gave up," Hogshead said. "I felt like I had done everything I could. I told him about my mother and how much she loved me. I told him I was pregnant. I told him I had a venereal disease. I told him everything I had read in *Seventeen Magazine* about what you're supposed to do to get yourself out of this kind of situation. I was trying to make him see me as a person. But I was losing. I was batting zero."

Hogshead, who did not go public with her ordeal until 1996, reported the rape to the police, but the assailant was never captured. Meanwhile, Hogshead tried to get back in the water when she was physically able, only to find out that the mental scars from her sexual assault were much more difficult to overcome. A fitness and health fanatic, Hogshead was known for eating properly and enduring grueling training sessions, in and out of the water. But her physical fitness could not compensate for the emotional damage inflicted by her rape.

After realizing that she needed time away, Hogshead left swimming for a little more than a year, fairly confident that she was not going to make a comeback. Eventually, Hogshead made her way back to the pool and competition for Duke, her reunion with the sport serving as a coping mechanism for her emotional pain. Additionally, Hogshead returned to the form that made her an elite competitor.

"It's much easier talking about this stuff at age 37 than at 19," Hogshead said in an interview years after her retirement,

I thought swimming was over for me after I got raped. I went through the feelings of being enraged. The why-me and where was God in all this? Physically, I could have gotten back in the water fairly quickly. But emotionally, no. I needed time to heal. I was scared to death every night, always checking the door to see if it was locked. I wasn't coping well. Once I did get back in the pool, swimming helped me work out my anger in a socially acceptable way. It was a sense of reclaiming my own body.

In 1983, Hogshead was named USA Swimming's Comeback Swimmer of the Year. It was a campaign that set the stage for Hogshead's qualification for the 1984 Games in the 100 freestyle, 200 butterfly, and 200 individual medley, along with two relays. At the same time that Hogshead was returning to action and coming to terms with her rape, Steinseifer was emerging as a star freestyler.

Like Hogshead and many female swimmers of the era, Steinseifer soared to major accolades early in her career. Steinseifer did not hail from one of the big-name club programs in the United States. Instead, she trained under Ken Belli with the West Valley Aquatic Team and became one of the small club's few national qualifiers.

It was clear at an early age that Belli and Steinseifer had excellent coach-swimmer chemistry, with Steinseifer qualifying for the 1983 Pan American Games. There, the 15-year-old Steinseifer won gold in the 100 freestyle and as a member of two U.S. relays. The win in the 100 freestyle immediately made her a leading challenger for Olympic gold, and she got that opportunity when she finished second at the U.S. Olympic Trials.

What made Steinseifer a scary opponent was her closing speed. Since Belli had her train more for the 200 freestyle, Steinseifer typically had a strong finish and was able to reel in tiring opponents down the stretch. It was a facet of her skill that ended up paying dividends in the Olympic final of the 100 freestyle.

In the Olympic Village in Los Angeles, Hogshead and Steinseifer were roommates and supportive of each other. Neither woman had any difficulty qualifying for the championship heat, but Steinseifer was not feeling in peak form, and doubts about her ability to succeed began to surface. "I remember thinking, 'Oh my God, I'm not even going to get a medal,'" Steinseifer said. "I felt terrible in the water." Of course, Steinseifer was being a bit melodramatic. When the women entered the water for the 100 freestyle final on July 29, Hogshead and the Netherlands' Annemarie Verstappen emerged at the front of the field, with Steinseifer lurking. Verstappen and Hogshead continued to duel into the second lap, with the Dutchwoman taking a lead until Hogshead started to battle back in the final 25 meters.

All along, Steinseifer remained unfazed and stuck with her race strategy. She never let Hogshead or Verstappen create too much of a gap, and in the final meters, it was Steinseifer who was gaining the most ground. As the swimmers touched the wall, that's when the confusion started to surface. While it was clear that Verstappen won the bronze medal, there was a "1" next to Steinseifer's name and a "2" aside Hogshead's. However, the American women were each listed with a time of 55.92.

Looking at the placement column, Steinseifer understandably engaged in a big celebration. "Carrie was over there hooting and hollering," Hogshead said. "And I just looked at her time and my time." Television commentary, which included former Olympic gold medalist Donna de Varona as an analyst, picked up on the confusion almost immediately, citing the fact that the times matched but not the placements. Eventually, a tie was announced, the first in swimming's Olympic history. Hogshead was the one who broke the news to her teammate.

"I didn't know we had tied," Steinseifer said. "I just saw the 1 and the 2 on the scoreboard. Then Nancy turned to me and said, 'We tied!' I'm glad it was a tie. To win in the Olympic Games is just great. I knew we were close, but not that close. I thought I'd slide back into my life. I don't think there was ever a 'normal' after that. There was a new normal."

The fact that Hogshead and Steinseifer were allowed to share the gold medal was the result of what unfolded in the 400 individual medley at the 1972 Olympics. At the finish between Sweden's Gunnar Larsson and American Tim McKee, the scoreboard showed the men to have tied. But officials reviewed the timing system and found that Larsson actually got to the wall two thousandths of a second quicker than McKee. From that point forward, it was decided that if athletes matched times to the hundredth of a second, they would be considered tied.

Only once since the tie between Hogshead and Steinseifer has there been a tie for the gold medal in Olympic swimming, and it was also in a sprint-freestyle event and between Americans. At the 2000 Games in Sydney, Gary Hall Jr. and Anthony Ervin jointly stood on the top step of the podium after posting identical times of 21.98 in the 50 freestyle.

The 100 freestyle was not the end of the Olympic experience for either woman. Hogshead and Steinseifer combined to help the United States to the gold medal in the 400 freestyle relay, and Hogshead added a gold medal in the 400 medley relay and a silver medal in the 200 individual medley. In her final event, the 200 butterfly, she just missed the podium for a fifth time, placing fourth.

Steinseifer went on to add national titles to her resume and was an NCAA champion at the University of Texas. But her quest for a second Olympiad ended poorly in 1988 when she struggled mightily and didn't come close to qualifying for the Seoul Games. "I don't know what happened," she said. "I swam better than I ever had at the NCAA [Championships] that year and felt really good about the Trials. I just had a bad week."

That was not the case in 1984, however, and Hogshead and Steinseifer are forever linked in Olympic lore. "This is the way I wanted it," Hogshead said. "This is the best experience of my life by far. It's like fantasyland."

CHART NO. 13.1

For more than 100 years, the Olympics have treated fans to countless memorable races. Still, some have stood above the rest, due to their down-to-the-wire finishes. Here is a look at the closest races in Olympic history, highlighted by a pair of gold medal ties.

Year	Site	Event	Gold Medalist	Silver Medalist	Time Difference
1984	Los Angeles	100 freestyle	Nancy Hogshead Carrie Steinseifer	None	Tie
2000	Sydney	50 freestyle	Gary Hall Jr. Anthony Ervin	None	Tie
1952	Helsinki	100 freestyle	Clarke Scholes	Hiroshi Suzuki	Tie[a]
1956	Melbourne	100 backstroke	Judy Grinham	Carin Cone	Tie[a]
1960	Rome	100 freestyle	John Devitt	Lance Larson	Tie[a]
1972	Munich	400 individual medley	Gunnar Larsson	Tim McKee	.002
1980	Moscow	200 butterfly	Ines Geissler	Sybille Schonrock	.01
1988	Seoul	100 breaststroke	Adrian Moorhouse	Karoly Guttler	.01
1988	Seoul	100 butterfly	Anthony Nesty	Matt Biondi	.01
1996	Atlanta	100 butterfly	Amy Van Dyken	Liu Limin	.01
2004	Athens	50 freestyle	Gary Hall Jr.	Duje Draganja	.01
2008	Beijing	50 freestyle	Britta Steffen	Dara Torres	.01
2008	Beijing	100 butterfly	Michael Phelps	Milorad Cavic	.01
2012	London	100 freestyle	Nathan Adrian	James Magnussen	.01

[a]Judges' decision.

Notes: At the 1952 Olympics, American Clarke Scholes and Japan's Hiroshi Suzuki posted matching times of 57.4, but officials used a judges' decision to award the gold medal to Scholes.

At the 1956 Olympics, Great Britain's Judy Grinham earned the gold medal via a judges' decision over American Carin Cone after they each were timed in 1:12.9.

In 1960, Australian John Devitt and the United States' Lance Larson both produced a time of 55.2, but a judges' decision gave the gold medal to Devitt and the silver medal to Larson. The United States filed an appeal of the decision but to no avail.

In the final of the 400 individual medley at the 1972 Olympics in Munich, Sweden's Gunnar Larsson was awarded the gold medal over the United States' Tim McKee after both men finished with times of 4:31.98. However, officials checked the timing system and found that Larsson touched the wall .002 ahead of McKee, thus handing the Swede the gold medal. Going forward, it was determined that if athletes finished tied to the hundredth of a second, they would share the place in which they finished without the time being extended to the thousandth of a second.

14

The Best of Biondi

When Matt Biondi walked away from the 1988 Games in Seoul with seven medals, including five gold, it was the best performance in the sport since Mark Spitz won seven gold medals at the 1972 Games.

Before Michael Phelps's name became synonymous with Mark Spitz, it was Matt Biondi who was measured against Spitz and what he achieved at the 1972 Olympic Games. At the 1988 Games in Seoul, Biondi did not match Spitz's seven–gold medal performance, but he won seven medals overall, including five gold, and left a legacy as one of the greatest performers in the sport's history.

The most-talked-about swimmer of the past 20 years is not difficult to identify. What Michael Phelps accomplished during his career, which launched on an international basis in 2000, is what greatness in the sport will be measured against for years to come. Considering Phelps's accumulation of 22 Olympic medals (including 18 gold) and 30-plus world-record performances, it might seem like an unfair measuring stick. After all, many pundits in the sport cannot foresee another Phelps ever emerging, such was the power of the man from Baltimore.

The same belief was held in the early 1970s when Mark Spitz capped his remarkable career with a showing for the ages at the 1972 Olympic Games in Munich. It was in Germany during an Olympiad as much remembered for tragedy as athletic prowess that Spitz won gold medals in each of his seven events, all in world-record time. As Spitz left for a whirlwind celebration/publicity tour, the consensus was that his exploits would never be matched.

Between the days of Spitz and the rise of the Phelps phenomenon, however, there was a bridge. His name was Matt Biondi, and for the second half of the 1980s and into the early 1990s, Biondi was the face of swimming. It was not a position with which Biondi was comfortable, for he preferred to fly undetected or at least as a minor blip on the radar. Yet, when an athlete possesses as much skill as Biondi, there is no escaping the spotlight, a fact that Biondi learned during the 1988 campaign. Entering the Seoul Games, nearly every discussion of Biondi and what he might achieve at the Olympics was linked to Spitz—specifically, whether he could match his 1972 Olympic output.

"I don't feel it's a fair comparison," said Biondi's coach, Nort Thornton.

> But people are going to do it. You can't stop them. It's unfortunate people get compared, but that's human nature. The rules have changed, and people can't swim as many events as they were able to in 1972. There are certain comparisons like the speed they both travel through the water, but Matt is definitely not Mark. He is his own swimmer. Someday people will be comparing another young swimmer to Matt. That's the way it works.

Biondi first surged onto the global scene when he somewhat surprisingly qualified for the 1984 Olympic Games in Los Angeles as a relay competitor. It was at a home Games in which the Southern California native captured a gold medal as a member of the U.S. 400 freestyle relay and ultimately started down a path that made Biondi one of the greats in his sport.

Blessed with natural sprinting speed yet enough endurance to stretch up to the 200-meter distance, Biondi was equally gifted as a freestyler and butterflyer. That overall combination allowed Biondi to embrace arduous schedules in major competition, usually a slate that included four individual events and duties with all three American relays. It was this agenda, pursued at the 1986 World Championships in Madrid, that significantly jump-started the hoopla surrounding Biondi's 1988 Olympic exploits.

At the fifth edition of the World Championships, Biondi walked away with seven medals—three gold, a silver, and three bronze. It wasn't nearly what Spitz pulled off, but it was enough to start the chatter and comparisons, which Biondi loathed.

"The burden of public expectation is tremendous," Biondi said.

It's like a ladder. When you start out, you're at the bottom and work up. There's satisfaction every time you climb one more rung. You see your accomplishments. The people keep getting smaller and smaller at the bottom. But when you reach the top, there's nowhere to go, only down. You feel stagnant. You look down and you have to fight people off. You lose a race and people sound as if you let them down. How could you do this to them?

When Biondi arrived in Seoul for the Games of the 24th Olympiad, he knew that the expectations were lofty and that the comparisons with Spitz would be a constant topic. Never mind that Biondi held only one individual world record entering the Games, as opposed to Spitz possessing world records in each of his four individual disciplines.

And forget the fact that the sport had grown internationally, with Biondi's competition spanning many more nations than that of Spitz. At the 1972 Games, only 10 countries managed medalists in men's swimming. When the 1988 Games concluded, 15 nations were represented on the medals podium. Despite these obstacles, the media and fans were clamoring for history and watching with a keen eye.

"I'd like to say something," Biondi wrote in a diary for *Sports Illustrated* during the Seoul Games.

I'm doing this diary because I want to voice the other side of the Olympics. Everyone will be counting the medals and the times and the world records, and making this big judgment: Is Matt a success or a failure? It seems there's so much emphasis put on that stuff and so little on how a person grows as he works his way toward the Olympics. To me, it's the path getting there that counts, not the cheese at the end of the maze. Having said that, I have to admit that I've got a case of prerace jitters right now. I want to win. After all, I've trained my whole career for this.

As soon as Biondi's Olympiad commenced, the chase for seven gold medals ended. Contesting the 200 freestyle, his weakest event, Biondi found himself up against a sterling field. For Biondi, the 200 freestyle was a reach. While his sprinting prowess was well suited for the 50 and 100 freestyles, he had to hold on for dear life in the 200 freestyle. As a way to compensate for what would be certain fading down the stretch, Biondi typically attacked the first half of the 200 free and hoped that his lead would be enough to prevail. It was a strategy that he employed in Seoul.

Dueling with the likes of West Germany's Michael Gross, the world-record holder, Australia's Duncan Armstrong, and Poland's Artur Wojdat, among others, Biondi bolted to the front of the field from the start. He held the lead at the 50-meter mark, sat second at the midway point, and was again in the lead at the final turn. But over the final 50 meters, Biondi gave way to his middle-distance foes and claimed the bronze medal behind Armstrong and Sweden's Anders Holmertz.

Armstrong's triumph was a major surprise, as he entered the event ranked 46th in the world. But Armstrong and his coach, Laurie Lawrence, assured that the Olympics would be the Australian's peak. Racing intelligently, Armstrong remained near the lane line and garnered a draft off of Biondi entering the last lap. His win set off one of the great celebrations by a coach in Olympic history.

In the stands for his pupil's race, Lawrence sweated every stroke with Armstrong. He walked up and down the steps, pounding a rolled-up program into his palm and covering his eyes and head at times with his hands and arms. When Armstrong touched the wall for the gold medal, Lawrence went berserk, eventually shaking a metal barricade so violently that South Korean police arrived out of concern for a major incident. Minutes later and still overly exuberant, Lawrence gave a love tap to the cheek of reporter Steven Quartermain during a television interview. As it turned out, the slap was so hard that it broke Quartermain's jaw.

If it wasn't the finish for which fans and the media yearned from Biondi, the American viewed the race as a strong start to his program. As far as he was concerned, a medal in his weakest discipline was only a positive and provided momentum for his remaining races. So, when others painted the performance as a failure, Biondi bristled at the notion. In fact, he personally expressed his displeasure to NBC Olympics anchor Bob Costas over a comment that Costas made during a studio show.

"I was happy: I swam the way I wanted to and beat the guys I thought I needed to, Gross and Wojdat," Biondi said in his *Sports Illustrated* diary.

> Duncan just had a hell of a swim. I had the lead and he stayed right on my shoulder, right by the lane line. I think he should buy me a beer or something because he probably got a pretty good draft from me.
>
> The press always throws stuff at you. Like tonight I heard Bob Costas say on TV, "Matt Biondi isn't going to win his seven gold medals. Today he had to settle for bronze." But I feel *good* about the bronze. My most difficult event is over, and I still have a chance to walk away with seven medals. I think that would be a hell of a performance.

As satisfied as Biondi was with his bronze medal from the 200 freestyle, his happiness turned to frustration in his next event. Biondi entered the 100 butterfly as the prohibitive favorite, in part because world-record-holder Pablo Morales failed to qualify for the Olympics at the U.S. Trials. Although the field featured Gross and Suriname's Anthony Nesty, Biondi was the man to beat.

As was his trademark in most of his events, Biondi pushed the pace from the start and made the turn under world-record pace. A superb turn only lengthened Biondi's edge on the field, and midway through the second lap, it seemed as if Biondi was competing against only the clock while in pursuit of the world record.

Even in the final meters, as the field tightened the gap, it still appeared as if Biondi would strike gold. But a poor finish proved costly. Faced with the decision to squeeze in an extra stroke or utilize a long glide to the wall, Biondi chose the latter option and stopped the clock in 53.01. Taking advantage of the opening provided by Biondi, Nesty had the perfect finish and got to the wall in 53.00, prevailing by the smallest of margins.

The look on Biondi's face at the end of the race spoke volumes. He wore a stunned expression and rolled his eyes, perfectly aware that the finish had erased what was—to that point—a sensational outing. This time, there would be no solace in a minor medal, only disappointment and self-questioning.

"I swam 99 meters like an Olympic champion," Biondi said. "I had been winning the race easily the whole way. It's been eating me up. After all, what's a 100th of a second? Could I have won with longer fingernails? A slightly quicker start? Looking at the tape of the race just makes me sick to my stomach."

For Nesty, his gold medal was the first (and remains the only) for his country in Olympic competition. Having moved to the United States to train at the Bolles School in Florida and eventually the University of Florida, Nesty threw his head back after the realization of his victory. It was in stark contrast to Biondi's reaction, although his mood changed a short time later.

Biondi had no time to dwell on his near miss, due to the 800 freestyle relay later in the night. Following the legs of Troy Dalbey, Matt Cetlinski, and Doug Gjertsen, Biondi came through with an anchor split of 1:46.44, the fastest in history. The effort not only enabled the United States to capture the gold medal but propelled the American squad to a world-record time of 7:12.51. It was also the start of a run of five straight gold medals by Biondi to punctuate his Seoul Games appearance.

Of all of Biondi's events, his next discipline was as close to a sure thing as it got. Biondi was largely viewed as unbeatable in the 100 freestyle. He was the world-record holder and had set the global standards on four occasions between 1985 and early 1988, with his mark of 48.42 from the 1988 Olympic Trials serving as one of the most jaw-dropping performances the sport had seen in some time.

Not surprisingly, Biondi had no trouble taking top honors in the 100 free, considered the blue-ribbon event in the sport. Biondi went through his two laps in an Olympic record of 48.63, almost a half second quicker than countryman Chris Jacobs and .99 faster than bronze medalist Stephan Caron of France.

"He was born with all the right tools," Thornton said of his athlete. "He has an incredible feel for the water. It's hard to describe. It's the same feel a pianist has for the keys and an artist's brush has for the canvas."

With Jacobs and Biondi bookending the U.S. 400 freestyle relay, which included Dalbey and Tom Jager on the middle legs, a third gold medal was draped around Biondi's neck. The foursome was timed in a world record of 3:16.53, which would last for nearly 7 years, but as soon as the medal ceremony ended, Biondi found himself no longer a teammate of Jager but his enemy.

Even today, more than a quarter century since the Seoul Games, the Biondi-Jager rivalry is revered as one of the best the sport has seen. Their clashes matched differing styles. While Biondi was a multievent star with range in the freestyle, Jager was a pure sprinter, a 50-meter specialist who could venture up to the 100 free for relay duty.

The 1988 Games marked the first time that the 50 freestyle was held in Olympic competition, but it was far from the first time that Biondi and Jager squared off for sizable stakes. They had met as collegiate athletes of the University of California—Jager for Los Angeles and Biondi for Berkeley—and they had met at the U.S. National Championships, each defeating the other. But in the lead-up to the Seoul Games, it was Jager who held the upper hand on the international scene.

At the 1986 World Championships, Jager stood atop the medals podium, with Biondi claiming the bronze. A year later at the Pan Pacific Championships, Jager again got the best of Biondi, who this time earned a silver. In Seoul, Jager would have easily sacrificed either of those crowns in exchange for Olympic gold.

Riding a huge wave of momentum, Biondi delivered a no-doubt-about-it win in the Olympic final, bolting to a noticeable lead at the midway point of the one-lap sprint. When Biondi hit the wall, the scoreboard flashed a time of 22.14, comfortably ahead of Jager's 22.36. Bronze medalist Gennadiy Prigoda of the Soviet Union was timed in 22.71, an eon behind for such a short race.

The normally reserved and stoic Biondi celebrated his victory over Jager with the most exuberance of his career. After realizing his triumph, Biondi thrust his fist into the air on several occasions and climbed on the lane rope with another fist pump. When it mattered most, he had gotten the best of his rival.

"The 50 free was it for me," Biondi said. "I have a picture of my reaction and it was the most jubilant I'd ever been. It was a world record. That swim made it for me."

Holding six medals, including four gold, the 400 medley relay was a curtain call of sorts for Biondi. As the United States roared to a 2-second-plus victory and its third world record in as many relay efforts, Biondi handled the butterfly leg on a squad that featured David Berkoff (backstroke), Richard Schroeder (breaststroke), and Jacobs (freestyle). It was the perfect cap to a scintillating stay in Seoul.

"I'll tell you, if someone had told me I was going to win five gold medals here and set or help to set four world records, I'd have jumped off my seat," Biondi said. "I'm very happy with my swims, except for the last yard of that 100 fly. Just think: It could have been six golds. But I accomplished what I set out to do, and now I can open a new chapter in my life."

In some ways, what Biondi achieved in Seoul is overlooked. The fact that he did not match Spitz's performance from Munich was a major storyline, and with Phelps's eight gold medals in Beijing and 18 gold medals throughout his Olympic career, it can be said Biondi was caught in the middle of the two biggest stars in swimming history.

For his part, Spitz was glad to see Biondi receive attention, in part because it was good publicity for the sport and partially due to his respect for Biondi's talents. It was also an opportunity for Spitz's name to return to the headlines, as was the case when Phelps embarked on his pursuit.

"I proved it could be done once and so that brought a lot of attention to Biondi," Spitz said.

> The press and the television were aware that I was in seven different events, [but] it wasn't until I got into my program and had won four or five medals that they started to realize that, "Hey, this guy could win it all." . . . Sure, in the back of my mind I guess I'm a little happy that the record is intact. But today is today and if he would have broken the record, I would have been happy, too.

Originally expected to leave the sport after the 1988 Games, Biondi returned from a sabbatical to compete in one more Olympiad. At the 1992 Games in Barcelona, he added three more medals to his career tally, taking gold in two relays and a silver in the 50 freestyle. The 11 medals that he accrued among the 1984, 1988, and 1992 Games rank among the most in Olympic history.

Still, what transpired in Seoul holds a special place in Biondi's heart. "It doesn't seem like 25 years ago because that sounds like a long time," Biondi said while reflecting on the 25th anniversary of his exploits. "To think of Seoul, I was able to distinguish myself not just in America, but as a great Olympian. That was my high watermark."

15

Nesty Nets Gold

When Anthony Nesty won the 100 butterfly at the 1988 Olympics in Seoul, prevailing by a hundredth of a second over American Matt Biondi, Nesty gave Suriname its first (and only) Olympic gold medal.

When Suriname's Anthony Nesty got his hands on the wall a hundredth of a second ahead of American Matt Biondi in the 100 butterfly at the 1988 Games in Seoul, it marked the first time that a black swimmer won a gold medal at the Olympic Games.

Because the truth should never get in the way of a good narrative, a British tabloid once chronicled Anthony Nesty's formative years in the sport with fantasy-film flair. Growing up in Suriname, Nesty was said to practice in swamps while evading the snapping jaws of crocodiles. The true-to-life Nesty tale isn't quite that heart pounding but nonetheless is a fabled story in swimming lore.

When Nesty first emerged on the international stage, his story stood out. Although he was a few years shy of becoming a world-class performer, there was enough potential evident in his 21st-place showing at the 1984 Olympics in Los Angeles to realize that a bright future awaited. Adding to the intrigue was Nesty's background. Not only did he hail from a tiny Caribbean country, Suriname, but his black heritage also made him a rarity in the sport.

In the mid-1980s, when Nesty's profile was rising, the closest that any black swimmer had come to winning an Olympic gold medal occurred at the 1976 Olympics in Montreal. In her second Olympiad, the Netherlands' Enith Brigitha had a pair of bronze medals draped around her neck. A decade later, minds started to wonder: Could Nesty take his ethnicity to the next athletic level by winning a gold medal?

If that scenario was to unfold, Nesty knew that he needed to pursue an avenue that led to aquatic stardom. Following his 1984 Olympic experience, Nesty moved to the United States and started to attend Florida's prestigious Bolles School, a prep school with a topflight reputation for producing elite swimmers.

By shifting his training ground to Bolles, Nesty began training under the watch of Gregg Troy, a move that proved to be one of the most beneficial events of his life on both a short- and long-term basis. His skills refined by Troy, Nesty placed fifth in the 100 butterfly at the 1986 World Championships and followed a year later by winning gold in the 100 fly at the Pan American Games. In a matter of 2 years, Nesty developed from young star to global force.

Although Nesty was a contender when the 1988 Games in Seoul rolled around, he was not the favorite. For starters, Nesty had to duel with American Matt Biondi, the biggest name in the sport and in pursuit of matching Mark Spitz's seven gold medals from the 1972 Games in Munich. Meanwhile, Germany's Michael Gross, the defending Olympic champion, was in the field, along with reigning European champion Andy Jameson of Great Britain.

Nesty wasn't rattled in the slightest. "I knew I had a chance to win the race," he said. "I knew I was going to be in the top three."

The confidence that Nesty possessed was a key when the final took place on the evening of September 21. As expected, Biondi bolted off the blocks and built a sizable lead, making the turn under world-record pace. As the athletes charged down the second lap, Biondi initially increased his lead and appeared unbeatable.

Even as Biondi tired toward the finish, he was still in command. That's when surprise set in. Nearing the wall, Biondi got caught in between strokes and had to make a decision whether to perform a few quick, choppy strokes or glide to the wall. He opted to glide, with Nesty nailing a near-perfect finish: Nesty got to the wall in 53.00, with Biondi behind by the slimmest of margins in 53.01. Nesty celebrated his triumph with a fist pump while Biondi wore a mixed look of disgust and shock.

"Going into the Olympics, I always felt I could make the finals," said Nesty, who has been a longtime assistant coach at his alma mater, the University of Florida.

> Any time you make the top eight, you have a chance. We tell our athletes, you have to put yourself in position to do well. My dad was there and it was a special moment. It was my second Olympics, and the first one didn't go so well. I was more prepared and fortunate enough to touch the wall first.
>
> It was an awesome experience. Any time you go to the Olympics and compete for your country, it's an honor and something you have for the rest of your life. In my case, I was fortunate enough to touch the wall first. Growing up in Suriname and as little kid going to all these Caribbean meets, you always dream of being the best in the world.

Taking down Biondi was no easy task. The Californian was racing a schedule that included the 100 fly and the 50, 100, and 200 freestyles, as well as all three relays, and in the months leading up to Seoul, Biondi was routinely compared to Spitz. Ultimately, Biondi won five gold medals, a silver, and a bronze. The silver medal is the one that displeased Biondi the most.

"I swam 99 meters like an Olympic champion, but couldn't fit in another stroke in the 100th meter," Biondi wrote in a diary he kept for *Sports Illustrated* during the 1988 Olympics.

> I was too close to the wall. I had to glide in, and Anthony Nesty of Suriname out-touched me. I had been winning the race easily the whole way. It's been eating me up. After all, what's a 100th of a second? Could I have won with longer fingernails? A slightly quicker start? Looking at the tape of the race just makes me sick to my stomach.

For Nesty, video of the race was nothing short of reliving a great moment. He became the first Olympic medalist from Suriname, and no one from his homeland in the quarter century since has been able to match him—in any sport. He also used the moment to bolster the profile of swimming in Suriname, with a huge jump in participation recognizable in the 10 to 12 years following his gold medal surge.

Although the initial jump in interest has waned some, swimming remains the most organized sport in Suriname, and Nesty returns home to conduct clinics as often as he can. During those visits home, he remains revered as an icon, dubbed a hero wherever he goes.

Following his Olympic crown, Nesty followed up with a world championship in the 100 butterfly in 1991 and three NCAA championships as a University of Florida standout. At the 1992 Olympics in Barcelona, Nesty was unable to defend his gold medal, which went to Pablo Morales, but Nesty stayed on the podium as the bronze medalist.

Several years later, Troy—who moved from the coach of Bolles to coach the University of Florida—tabbed Nesty to join his staff. In their time together, Troy and Nesty have continued to enjoy tremendous success, highlighted by the mentoring of numerous NCAA individual champions and guiding the Florida women's program to an NCAA team title in 2010.

"Anthony is one of the most revered coaches in college swimming, and one of the few who is considered both a great athlete and a great coach," Troy said. "He's got a great work ethic and a tremendous ability to get results. His experience at the Olympics as an athlete is instrumental in his ability to relate to our current athletes, and his reputation for getting the most out of them speaks for itself."

Quiet by nature, Nesty doesn't often think about his moment of Olympic glory. If he does, it's that someone asked a question about 1988 or prodded him into reliving that special day in his career. Otherwise, Nesty is thrilled with his role as a coach and working with his athletes to produce their best results.

"I don't think of it much, but I know my place in history," he said.

> My philosophy is that I had a great career as an athlete, but my goal now is to be the best coach I can be for the athletes [at the University of Florida]. That said, it's obviously a great honor, especially when I go to Suriname. They're still celebrating after 25 years and it's such a sense of pride for a small country like Suriname, and everyone who had a hand in my success should feel a sense of pride.

No, Nesty's story does not include a chapter on racing away from crocodiles in swampy waters, as once suggested. But it's still a tale of intrigue.

16

The Dragon Slayer

Ranked 46th in the world in the 200 freestyle entering the 1988 Olympic Games in Seoul, Australia's Duncan Armstrong was an afterthought in medal discussions. When the championship final was over, however, Armstrong was the gold medalist, and his stunning triumph set off one of the great coaching celebrations that the sport has seen.

Wherever Duncan Armstrong looked, he had reason to be in awe. From what he heard, he had reason to be in awe, too. It was the championship final of the 200 freestyle at the 1988 Olympic Games in Seoul, South Korea, and Armstrong was supposed to be an also-ran in a clash of titans.

Next to Armstrong was the United States' Matt Biondi, the world's most dominant swimmer of the time and—prior to arriving in Seoul—tabbed as a threat to equal the seven gold medals won by Mark Spitz at the 1972 Games in Munich. As the meet announcer introduced Biondi, set to compete in lane 5, it seemed like a dissertation was being read. Accolade followed accolade. If spectators somehow did not know Biondi before his introduction, they were well versed on his accomplishments afterward.

Also behind a starting block was West Germany's Michael Gross, nicknamed "The Albatross" for his 7-foot wingspan. Like Biondi, Gross was wildly decorated, an Olympic champion from 4 years earlier and a world titlist on multiple occasions. He headed into the final of the 200 freestyle as the world-record holder, a mark that he set en route to the gold medal at the 1984 Games.

In another lane was Poland's Artur Wojdat. Although not as esteemed as Biondi and Gross, Wojdat was quite accomplished. He was the world-record holder in the 400 freestyle and was viewed as a future star in the sport, a man who was just tapping into his potential.

Then there was Armstrong, a Commonwealth Games champion for Australia 2 years earlier but hardly of the same status as his fellow competitors. He ranked just 46th in the world in the 200 freestyle at the time of the Olympic Games, and when it was time for Armstrong's introduction in Seoul, it was basically over as soon as it started. Little was said, prompting Armstrong to think, "Oh, come on!" More, Armstrong didn't exactly possess an imposing physique. While Gross was a towering 6-foot-7 and armed (literally) with a propeller-like wingspan, Biondi looked like a sculptor's dream creation, himself 6-foot-7 and rippling with muscles. Armstrong? He was built nothing like an Adonis. Rather, he was an unimposing 6-foot-2 and 160 pounds.

If Armstrong was not a contender in many minds, Laurie Lawrence was unaware that his student was an underdog. One of the finest coaches in Australian history, Lawrence saw great potential in Armstrong. Physically, he drove Armstrong into the ground in training, providing a new definition of what was painful. Equally important, Lawrence influenced Armstrong on a mental level, convincing his charge that excellence was attainable. It was that mentality that allowed Armstrong to believe—if others did not—that guys like Biondi and Gross were beatable.

"He's a wonderful and enthusiastic person," Armstrong said of Lawrence.

He just sells it. He sells passion. He's a wonderful man. In swimming, where you have to do hundreds and hundreds and hundreds of laps, passion and enthusiasm are very important. He really understood the Olympic equation that you only get one shot. The door of opportunity only opens once every four years. He gave you the tools of the trade to step on deck so the Olympic pressure would not crush you. You look down your lane and know you've done everything you possibly can and you're prepared for this race. Someone has got to win it. Why not me? You go out against great opposition and perform your best and not let the pressure cooker crush you.

The pressure cooker is what Biondi was under. In the 16 years since Spitz packaged the finest Olympic performance in history—seven gold medals and seven world records—the sport was waiting for someone to challenge that epic run. Biondi was that man. He was slated to race seven events—four individual and three relays—and the potential for a gold medal in each event certainly existed.

Of all the events, however, the 200 freestyle was going to be the toughest for Biondi, who was more of a sprinter extending his talent as far as it would go. In the case of the 200 freestyle, that was four grueling laps against athletes who were primarily middle-distance performers. While Biondi knew the situation and while fans in tune with the sport understood the task at hand, the casual follower saw the 200 freestyle as nothing more than a fragment of a seven-piece puzzle.

"I'd like to say something," Biondi wrote for *Sports Illustrated*.

I'm doing this diary because I want to voice the other side of the Olympics. Everyone will be counting the medals and the times and the world records, and making this big judgment: Is Matt a success or a failure? It seems there's so much emphasis put on that stuff and so little on how a person grows as he works his way toward the Olympics. To me, it's the path getting there that counts, not the cheese at the end of the maze. Having said that, I have to admit that I've got a case of prerace jitters right now. I want to win. After all, I've trained my whole career for this.

Armstrong, too, wanted nothing more than to win, and he might have been in a more advantageous position to get the job done. While Biondi and Gross were under enormous pressure, Armstrong was in a nothing-to-lose position. It was a scenario that paid tremendous dividends.

As the 200 freestyle started, Armstrong immediately put himself in contention. While Biondi had the lead at the 50-meter mark and Sweden's Anders Holmertz was in front at the midway point, Armstrong was lurking—and his coach knew it. A nervous wreck in the stands, Lawrence paced and fidgeted throughout the race. With a rolled-up program in his hands, Lawrence repeatedly pounded his hand with the paperwork or waved it in the air. Armstrong was where Lawrence wanted him to be.

During the third lap, Armstrong remained near the front of the pack, not losing touch with the leaders. As the athletes hit the 150-meter mark, Biondi had regained the lead and was one lap from collecting what would be the most difficult gold medal. Armstrong, though, produced a sterling final turn, one he called a "cracker," and he was suddenly even with Biondi. A few strokes later, Armstrong was ahead. As the swimmers charged through the final 15 meters, Armstrong was clearly in front and ended up securing the gold medal with a world record time of 1:47.25. Holmertz managed to clip Biondi for the silver medal, with Biondi fending off Wojdat and Gross for the bronze medal.

"I finished third in a great 200 (freestyle) behind Holmertz and Duncan Armstrong of Australia, who broke Gross' world record with a 1:47.25," Biondi wrote in his *Sports Illustrated* diary.

> I was happy. I swam the way I wanted to and beat the guys I thought I needed to, Gross and Wojdat. Duncan just had a hell of a swim. I had the lead and he stayed right on my shoulder, right by the lane line. I think he should buy me a beer or something because he probably got a pretty good draft from me.
>
> The press always throws stuff at you. Like tonight I heard Bob Costas say on TV, "Matt Biondi isn't going to win his seven gold medals. Today he had to settle for bronze." But I feel *good* about the bronze. My most difficult event is over, and I still have a chance to walk away with seven medals. I think that would be a hell of a performance.

A hell of a performance is the only way to describe what Armstrong pulled off. He celebrated the greatest triumph of his career with a few fist pumps and extended his arms over his head. Australian fans in the stands reveled in the moment. They had just witnessed an improbable triumph, a victory that required Armstrong to produce a perfect race—physically and tactically.

As excited as Armstrong was with his career-defining moment, his celebration did not compare to the jubilation expressed by Lawrence. At the 1984 Olympics in Los Angeles, Lawrence had mentored teenager Jon Sieben to the gold medal in the 200 butterfly, a victory that happened to come at the hands of Gross. Sieben charged down the last lap of that race and set a world record to grab the gold medal. Four years later, it was Armstrong who stormed down the final lap, defeated Gross, among others, and set a world record. Both men raced out of lane 6 in the championship final, a fact not lost on Lawrence, who repeatedly screamed, "Lucky lane 6!"

The longtime coach acted more like a caged animal than a human as he enjoyed Armstrong's moment briefly with spectators before losing control. He walked up and down the steps of the stands, seemingly unsure what to do. He yelled. He shook a metal barrier along a walkway in the stands, prompting South Korean police to make their way to Lawrence, who assured them that he was all right. As Armstrong made his way to the podium for the medals ceremony, Lawrence called down to his pupil a number of times, "Hey, Dunc. I know you." That repeated calling got the attention of Biondi, who leaned toward Armstrong during the medal ceremony and asked for an explanation. Armstrong wryly informed Biondi—who ultimately totaled five gold medals, a silver, and a bronze—that the crazy man was his coach. Lawrence simply could not contain his joy.

Still, nothing matched the first interview that Lawrence gave immediately after Armstrong's win. Approached by Australian television journalist Steven Quartermain, Lawrence was asked one of the most common questions following a historic moment, the old "how do you feel?" query.

"Mate, we just beat three world-record holders," an elated Lawrence yelled at Quartermain. "How do you think I feel? What do you think we come for, mate? Silver? Stuff the silver. We come for the gold."

During his answer and without any malicious intent, Lawrence slapped Quartermain on the side of the face a few times. It was supposed to be a love tap, one of those caught-in-the-moment situations. But Lawrence was so excited and on such an adrenaline rush that his slaps were hard enough to break Quartermain's jaw.

Armstrong's victory and Lawrence's celebratory antics are highlighted in Bud Greenspan's documentary *Favorite Stories of Olympic Glory*. Greenspan is considered one of the foremost Olympic experts in history, and in the documentary, Armstrong and Lawrence cherish and laugh about their moment of glory. Quartermain, too, recalls the impromptu interview that resulted in his facial trauma. It is a sensational package that sums up the meaning of the Olympic spirit, hard work, and the meaningful partnership between athlete and coach.

Later in the week, Armstrong added a silver medal in the 400 freestyle, an achievement that only added to his Olympic legacy. In the years since, he has been a motivational speaker, telling others about the importance of focus, belief, and dedication.

"It was [a feeling] of more relief than anything else because we had trained four or five years for that moment and the race takes less than two minutes," Armstrong said.

> You go two minutes on one day every four years. That's the clock. You do an enormous amount of training and then you get there and we had the perfect race. We had the great strategy and some good competition in the water. We had a world record. All my dreams and hopes in swimming came true in one touch of the wall. It was just wonderful. It was the perfect moment for us. It was the pinnacle of my swimming career.

17

A Tale of Redemption

After stunningly missing out on the 1988 Olympics in Seoul, Pablo Morales embarked on one of the greatest comebacks in the sport's history, a tale which was punctuated by a gold medal in the 100 butterfly at the 1992 Games in Barcelona.

*After failing to qualify for the 1988 Games in Seoul as the heavy favorite in the 100
butterfly, Pablo Morales retired and began pursuit of a law degree. However, the urge to
compete again grabbed Morales ahead of the 1992 Games, which turned into a fairy tale
when Morales claimed the gold medal in his prime event.*

The initial end—or what was perceived to be the end—was not one of those feel-
good tales that captures fans' hearts. It was quite the opposite, actually, a brutal finish
to what had otherwise been a remarkable career. While athletes in some sports can
get away with a subpar performance, rarely does swimming allow that luxury.

Think of the baseball diamond and the numerous times that we have heard about
a pitcher working his way to a victory without his best "stuff." Maybe his curveball
doesn't feature its typical bite, but the ability to lean on pinpoint location or intel-
ligent pitch selection enables the pitcher to fake his way through a start and to a win.

A stopwatch sport such as swimming plays by different rules. Because the clock
doesn't lie, athletes at less than their optimal level are cruelly left to wonder: "What
happened? Why was I slower than the last time out? Why did everything fall apart
now, at the very moment that I needed to be at the top of my game?" Sometimes,
the answers are hard to find. Sometimes, that is just the way it is. Ask Pablo Morales.

The son of Cuban-born parents, Pedro and Blanca, Morales was introduced to
swimming at a young age, largely because his mother had a near-drowning experience before moving to the United States and wanted her child to have water awareness. Although brought to the sport for safety reasons, Morales almost immediately
showed a tremendous feel for the water.

It was not long before Morales had developed a strong reputation as an elite performer on the junior level and earned a scholarship to compete for the high-powered
program at Stanford University. As a collegiate athlete, Morales became a global
phenomenon. Just after his freshman year at Stanford, Morales broke a world record
in the 100 butterfly at the U.S. Olympic Trials and then won three medals at the
1984 Games in Los Angeles.

"[My parents] worked really hard so that they could provide that for us," Morales
said. "I think because of that, we lived fairly comfortably and we were able to dream
big. And I was fortunate that I latched on to something that I did fairly well and I
was driven to do."

Morales's own words do not do justice to his vast talent. While a retaliatory boycott by the Eastern Bloc nations diluted the talent at the 1984 Olympics, as was the
case when the United States boycotted the 1980 Games in Moscow, it was still a
launching ground for Morales. He won silver medals in both the 100 butterfly and
200 individual medley and helped the American squad capture the gold medal in
the 400 medley relay.

His meeting with West Germany's Michael Gross in the 100 butterfly marked the
first of several clashes. Widely considered the best swimmer in the world at the time,
Gross needed the perfect performance to better Morales in Los Angeles, which is
exactly what he delivered with a world-record effort of 53.08. Morales was also under

the previous world record, going 53.23, and as a 19-year-old, there was little doubt that Morales was on the verge of greatness, perhaps as one of the finest swimmers produced by the United States.

By the end of 1985, Morales had picked up a pair of individual gold medals—in the 100 butterfly and 200 individual medley—at the Pan Pacific Championships, outings that led to a superb 1986 campaign. Not only did Morales reclaim his world record in the 100 butterfly, but his swim of 52.84 endured as the global standard for 9 years. More, Morales won his first world title, prevailing in the 100 butterfly ahead of American teammate Matt Biondi. He followed in 1987 with another 100 fly win at the Pan Pacific Championships.

All along, Morales was sculpting—arguably—the finest collegiate career ever produced by a man. En route to leading Stanford to three NCAA team championships, Morales won the 100 and 200 butterflies in each of his four seasons, as well as the 200 individual medley in his final 3 years. The 11 individual NCAA crowns made Morales the most decorated male swimmer in college history, having bettered the 10 titles won by the University of Southern California's John Naber in the 1970s.

Considering the momentum built by Morales on both the international and collegiate stages, there was little reason to doubt his qualification for the 1988 Olympic Games in Seoul. But as the U.S. Trials in Austin, Texas, approached, Morales took a measured approach to the selection meet.

With only the top-two individuals selected for the Olympics in each event, the Trials are considered by many to be more pressure packed than the Games. Third place is no better than last, and a hundredth of a second can be the difference for a lifelong dream coming to fruition or shattering into pieces. For many years, the third-place finisher at the American Trials would have contended for the Olympic podium.

"There are a lot of people who second-guess our system because it pays no special regard to world-record holders," Morales said heading to the 1988 Trials. "Other countries assure their stars of a place on the team. But our system gives the late bloomers a chance. It puts you in a similar situation to what you'll face at the Olympic Games. Swimmers must perform under that pressure. It's hit or miss, do or die. But that's the kind of athlete the U.S. wants in the Olympic Games."

For Morales, the Lee & Joe Jamail Swim Center on the campus of the University of Texas became a disastrous setting. After moving into the final of the 100 butterfly as the No. 2 seed, Morales was denied a trip to Seoul in the final of his best event. More than a half second off his world record, Morales finished behind Biondi and Jay Mortenson in what remains one of the biggest surprise misses in U.S. Trials history. Morales followed with another third-place finish in the 200 butterfly and did not advance out of the preliminaries of the 200 individual medley.

The end of his career—so it seemed—came earlier than expected. Morales was not the only person surprised by the results. His shortcoming was the talk of the Trials, so much so that several coaches spoke of their desire to see Morales on the American squad. While Morales was a Team USA veteran and leader, he was also one of the most likeable swimmers in the country.

"You're thinking that you have a chance to make the Olympic team, but then all of a sudden there's a really stark, abrupt ending to one's swimming career," Morales said.

> It's over. Boom. You're done. Because you don't think you're going on another four years. The 100-meter butterfly is my forte. It has been throughout my entire career. I felt it was my best shot to make the team. Over the years, I've taken a great deal of pride in this event and . . . that's the type of meet it is. Favorites don't always make it. Underdogs surprise you. That's the beauty of this meet.

When Morales left Austin, he also left his sport behind. He traveled East, started law school at Cornell University, and began eating without care, a decision that caused the disappearance of a once well-defined body. For 3 years, he was away from the pool—the place that had yielded so much success and joy but also some real pain.

About a year before the Barcelona Games, Morales's mother lost her battle with cancer, and Morales lost one of the most important people in his life. As she was dying, he decided to give the sport one final go, to see if he could rekindle any of his past magic. He knew there were no guarantees, but this journey was one that he wanted to undertake.

Working with his college coach, Skip Kenney, Morales had to get into shape in a short period. Fortunately, he was able to make large gains, and he realized early on in his comeback that his decision was the correct one. He had to try. "The key for me was realizing whether it was something I truly wanted to do again," Morales said.

> And once I got back into it again, I was like, "Oh, this is right. This is good. This is what I wanted to do." It was wonderful being back in the water again and training, getting in shape and having that quantifiable goal to go after.
>
> I just decided in August after my mom died I wanted to give it another try. I was older and more mature. I could handle failure. When someone you love dies, the pain and sense of loss, it never really goes away. That was a very difficult time for us. My mom was very supportive of my swimming career and it was very meaningful for her. . . . I'd actually decided to make a comeback prior to her passing away. She knew about it.

Morales's performance at the U.S. Trials in Indianapolis was a fairy tale of sorts. Although he was more than a second slower than his world record, Morales qualified for the 1992 Games in Barcelona by finishing first in the 100 butterfly, a hundredth of a second quicker than Mel Stewart. Fellow competitors were overjoyed to see Morales back on the Olympic Team.

In the stands, Pedro Morales held a picture of his wife and Pablo's mother in the air as his son secured a berth to Barcelona. The image was touching, and tears flowed freely among members of the Morales family and beyond. Yet, qualifying was just the first stage of Morales's journey. Once he qualified, there was no reason to believe that he couldn't add another chapter to his comeback tale.

"I'd never count out somebody as talented as Pablo," said Mark Schubert, who guided the U.S. women at the 1992 Games.

But I thought it was going to be a real tough comeback. Then, I saw him swim at the U.S. Open meet in December and it was obvious that he was going to get himself really fit and that the talent was still there. I think the sky's the limit. I think he can accomplish anything. . . . He'll definitely be near his best time, if not better, and that should be good enough. Everybody on the team wants him to succeed. There's nobody that the team feels deserves it more than him.

As Barcelona approached, Morales was frequently asked about what took place 4 years earlier, about the death of his mother and about his comeback dreams. Legendary Olympic historian and documentarian Bud Greenspan even had cameras following Morales for an upcoming documentary on the Barcelona Games. Never did Morales try to be anyone but himself. On the night of the 100 butterfly in Seoul, Morales admitted to leaving the room when the event came on television.

"During the Seoul Olympics, I really didn't watch much of the Games, which, for me, is unusual because I'm a very big sports fan," Morales said. "I enjoy an athletic spectacle such as the Olympic Games. I did catch a little of the Games, but I didn't watch my race. It wasn't my race. Sorry about that. It's melodramatic, I know, but it hurt not to be there."

Some of the competition that Morales knew during his heyday was gone by the summer of 1992. Gross retired after the previous year's World Championships, and Biondi was no longer contesting the 100 butterfly. Still, when Morales climbed the blocks in Barcelona, he wasn't working against a weak field. Suriname's Anthony Nesty returned as the defending Olympic champion, and Poland's Rafal Szukala was a European champion.

Known for his early speed, Morales had the lead at the turn, and while he started to fade at the finish, he found the wall early enough to fend off Szukala, with Nesty on the podium for a second straight Olympiad with the bronze medal. After hitting the wall, Morales recognized an atmosphere similar to 1984, when he placed second to Gross.

"This was my time at last," Morales said.

I guess I wanted to hear a reaction first before I turned around. There is a moment of silence, and it was eerily reminiscent of the silence I heard at the 1984 Games, when the crowd was silent except for the German contingent when Michael Gross had won. I wasn't going to turn around too quickly. I wanted to gather my composure and then turn around to see the scoreboard. I searched for my name and looked for the numbers.

I was prepared not to win this race. You imagine every possible outcome: winning, losing, not making finals. The reason I came back was for the Olympic experience. This is an arena where the best come together, each with a dream of winning a gold medal. Every athlete really yearns for a competition such as this. That's something that's always been within me, even though I had a preoccupation with legal studies. I know it was always within me.

The thrill of Morales's victory grabbed headlines in *Sports Illustrated* and major newspapers around the United States. The significance of his triumph also affected former rivals, including Gross.

"I cried when he won," Gross said. "I have wanted him to win a gold medal ever since I beat him."

Before the Barcelona Games, Morales was viewed as a great in U.S. swimming lore. He was an Olympic medalist, a world-record holder, and an NCAA legend. But after Morales conquered the world in 1992, his story took on a fairy-tale quality, elevating his status further. His tale had a bit of everything: a comeback from vast disappointment set against the backdrop of family grief.

"Given that 3 years away from the sport, I think I was able to achieve a certain sort of perspective about why I trained, why I was a competitive swimmer," said Morales, who has spent more than a decade as the head coach of the women's program at the University of Nebraska.

> For me, the greatest source of fulfillment was setting a goal and making progress toward achieving that goal. People were affected by the comeback. I looked at going to the Olympics as a chance for glory and fulfillment. That is what every athlete is seeking, a chance to prove himself on one day against the best competition in his sport. That is the ultimate.

18

Gold Medal Guitar

Confident in his team's ability to win the 400 freestyle relay at the 2000 Olympics, the always outspoken Gary Hall Jr. declared the United States would defeat Australia. Hall proved to be inaccurate, as the Aussies won in front of their home fans and handed the Americans their first loss in the event in Olympic competition.

*Before the 2000 Olympic Games in Sydney, the United States had never lost the 400
freestyle relay in Olympic competition, thus allowing Gary Hall Jr. to claim that the
Americans would smash the upstart Australians like guitars. After the race, the Aussies
were strumming along to their national anthem.*

Bulletin board fodder is part of the fabric of athletics. As long as newspapers, magazines, and, more recently, websites have reported on sporting events, athletes have
been warned to steer clear of partaking in trash talk. More than anyone, coaches have
given the "play nice" directive, concerned that any out-of-line chatter could provide
unnecessary motivation for the competition.

Of course, some athletes just can't help themselves. From the football field to the
basketball court and even in the pool, certain athletes lose control of their lips or
simply have no desire to keep them sealed. In this category, swimming counts Gary
Hall Jr. among the brashest athletes the sport has known.

No one can dispute Hall's talents. He is a 10-time Olympic medalist, including
back-to-back champion in the 50 freestyle in 2000 and 2004, and he is recognized
as a man who saved his finest outings for the biggest stage. During his career, it was
common for Hall to lay low in non-Olympic years, only to rise again when the biggest glory was on the line.

As talented as Hall was in the water, he was equally recognized for his showman-
ship and quotable nature. His prerace routine featured walks to the starting blocks
in a robe and American flag–colored boxing shorts, with a shadow-boxing show to
follow—and that was only the physical part of his demeanor.

Verbally, Hall never held back either. On several occasions, he exchanged barbs
with his Russian rival Alexander Popov, widely considered the greatest sprint freestyler in history. He also fired off shots at American teammates, including allegations
that Olympic champion Amy Van Dyken used performance-enhancing drugs.

So, when Hall voiced his opinions about the United States' clash with Australia in
the 400-meter freestyle relay at the 2000 Olympic Games in Sydney, it was hardly
surprising that his comments were colorful.

"I like Australia, in truth. I like Australians," Hall said in an Olympic diary he
kept for CNNSI.com.

> The country is beautiful, and the people are admirable. Good humor and genuine kind-
> ness seem a predominant characteristic. My biased opinion says that we will smash them
> like guitars. Historically the U.S. has always risen to the occasion. But the logic in that
> remote area of my brain says it won't be so easy for the United States to dominate the
> waters this time. Whatever the results, the world will witness great swimming.

On the whole, Hall's comments were gracious toward Australia and those whom
he was set to face on the Olympic stage. But the words found in the middle of his
statement stood out most. When Hall indicated that the United States would "smash
them like guitars," a feud was stirred. It was exactly the bulletin board material that
coaches pray they don't see from their athletes.

To understand Hall's brashness and confidence, all one needs is a history lesson on the United States' success in the 400 freestyle relay in international competition. The event was added to the Olympic program in 1964, and leading up to the 2000 Games, the United States was seven-for-seven in pursuit of gold medals, with limited opposition on the way to perfection. Meanwhile, from 1973 to 1998, American squads were eight-for-eight in claiming gold in the 400 freestyle relay at the World Championships.

With legends such as Don Schollander, Mark Spitz, Rowdy Gaines, and Matt Biondi powering this previous success, a loss by the United States in an international 400 freestyle relay was difficult to fathom. Could it actually happen? At least one country believed that the feat was plausible.

Dating to the days of Dawn Fraser and Murray Rose, Australia long boasted a rich swimming tradition. Although significantly smaller than the United States in population, Australia established itself as an aquatic superpower, earning its share of international plaudits. Still, a win over the United States in an American stranglehold was going to be a stretch—until a certain youngster emerged as a man who would carry his country and the sport for several years.

At the 1998 World Championships, Ian Thorpe made history by winning gold in the 400 freestyle as a 15-year-old. He was immediately pegged as a superstar, someone who could be the greatest ever. With a home Olympiad just 2 years away, a buzz was generated. Australia had a chance to do something special on its soil.

As the Sydney Games rolled around, there was no shortage of attention placed on Thorpe. Scheduled to contest the 200 and 400 freestyles and three relays, the Thorpedo, as he was nicknamed, was deemed a contender for five medals, perhaps all gold. It wouldn't take long for the 17-year-old to stand under the spotlight.

The first night of action in Sydney was a busy one for Thorpe, as he had to race the 400 freestyle before handling the anchor leg of the 400 freestyle relay. As difficult as that double may have been, it was a blessing for the Australians, given what transpired in the 400 freestyle.

For Thorpe—already the world-record holder and reigning world champion—the 400 freestyle was a coronation of sorts. For eight laps, he put the 17,000 fans in the Sydney Aquatic Centre into a frenzied state. Standing and screaming, the Aussie crowd watched Thorpe blow away his foes, his size-17 feet propelling him to a world record of 3:40.59, which was good for victory by nearly 3 seconds over Italian Massimiliano Rosolino.

Thorpe's victory also generated considerable momentum for the evening's final event, the 400 freestyle relay. The fans knew what was at stake, and they deeply wanted the squad of Michael Klim, Chris Fydler, Ashley Callus, and Thorpe to do something never before accomplished in Olympic history: beat the Americans in the 400 freestyle relay. Of course, the Aussies themselves wanted gold, and they were well aware of Hall's words.

"We came down to the lobby, and there it was on the front page of the paper," Klim said of Hall's infamous words from his diary. "To be totally honest, we really didn't take it too seriously and despite what people think, it wasn't really motivating for us. We knew we were walking into something that was going to be incredibly tough. The Americans had never been beaten at the Olympics and were world-record holders."

It was Klim who ignited the Australians with the start they needed. Leading off opposite American Anthony Ervin, Klim blazed through his two laps like no man previously, clocking a world record for the 100 freestyle with a leg of 48.18. With Ervin checking in at 48.89, Klim immediately put the Australians in command, while the United States fell vulnerable in an event where vulnerability was foreign. As impressive as it was, Klim's leadoff leg became even more daunting in retrospect.

Fydler and Neil Walker went into the water second for their respective nations, and Walker was able to slice 17 hundredths off the U.S. deficit before turning things over to Jason Lezak, who 8 years later would be the hero of the 400 freestyle relay at the Beijing Olympics. With a split 29 hundredths swifter than what Callus managed, the Americans pulled closer to the Australians heading into the final lap, where Thorpe and Hall would duel.

"Standing on the blocks, you know how calm Thorpie is," Klim said while reliving the event years later.

> I needed to get him fired up because we needed him to go out faster than he ever had before. I was just screaming, "You can do it Thorpie. No pain. No fear." I was screaming crap, but it worked.
>
> He went out well but still Gary Hall swam past him. We couldn't exactly tell how far he was behind at the turn but we knew he was up against it. Then at the 25-meter mark he started to motor and his kick picked up, but he was still behind. It was only in the last 10 meters he almost kicked into that other gear, Gary Hall faded, and we had beaten them and broken the world record.
>
> It's funny but when I do talks to groups of people and show that relay, people start cheering while watching that last leg. And I often hear people say, "I remember exactly where I was that night." It's nice to have that place in history.

Indeed, Hall surged ahead of Thorpe during the first lap of the anchor leg, providing hope that the United States would extend its unbeaten streak in the event. But with Hall a pure sprinter and Thorpe a middle-distance star, Thorpe figured to come back on Hall down the stretch—exactly the scenario that unfolded. At the wall, the Aussies had the gold medal in 3:13.67 and the Americans the silver in 3:13.86, both nations under the previous world record by more than a second.

Since Hall actually outsplit Thorpe on the anchor leg, the United States had faster splits on all but the opening leg, which is why the aforementioned retrospect comes into play. It was Klim's world record off the start and the cushion that he provided that proved to be the difference in Australia snapping the Americans' dominance in the event. Another key was Thorpe swimming a smart leg and not panicking when Hall bolted ahead during the early stages of their clash.

"I'd be a liar if I said it wasn't somewhat disappointing," Hall said.

In the same breath, I'd say we were close to a second under the world record. It's nothing to be ashamed of. Tonight was something the swimming world has never seen before. The last 50 meters were rather painful. I went after it. This is the Olympics, all or nothing. I doff my swimming cap to the great Ian Thorpe. He had a better finish than I had.

Although Klim indicated that Hall's comments weren't motivating when the Australians saw the press clippings the morning of the race, the celebration told a different story. After Thorpe touched the wall first and reached out of the water to accept congratulations from his teammates, the Australians broke into an impromptu jam session.

Responding to Hall's comment that the Australians would be smashed like guitars, Klim led his teammates in an air-guitar performance that was thoroughly enjoyed by the raucous crowd. A changing of the guard had taken place.

"I think it was [Fydler] who suggested it," Klim said.

We whispered in each other's ears, "let's do the air guitars." That wasn't planned nor had we spoken about it. Hadn't been mentioned at all, but on the spur of the moment we did it. But I must say, Gary Hall was the first swimmer to come over and congratulate us. Even though he dished it out, he was a true sportsman.

We had the presentation, then drug testing, then headed back to the village. I still remember walking into the dining hall, it was about midnight, maybe later, but there were still maybe 200 people there and we got a standing ovation. For the next two days wherever we went we were getting standing ovations.

The setback for the United States marked the end of its invincibility in the event. It failed to win gold at the 2001 and 2003 World Championships, and at the 2004 Games in Athens, the Americans dropped to the bronze medal. The 2008 Games brought a return of gold, thanks to Lezak producing the greatest relay split in history to overhaul France, but the French got revenge at the 2012 Olympics in London, with the United States taking silver.

Although the United States has been unable to maintain the dominance that it boasted leading into the 2000 Olympics, it is not indicative of a major drop-off in American talent. Rather, Australia used its victory to prove that other nations had the talent to compete with the best, provided all its parts worked as a harmonious unit.

For Hall, he flew under the radar from 2001 to 2003, uninterested in the two World Championships that preceded the Athens Games of 2004. When it was time to defend his gold medal in the 50 freestyle in Athens, Hall delivered under pressure. Of course, he found his way into controversy, too. It wouldn't be a Gary Hall–attended meet otherwise, would it?

As the U.S. coaching staff contemplated its lineup for the 400 freestyle relay, Hall had choice words when Michael Phelps was selected for the relay despite not contesting the 100 freestyle at the U.S. Trials. At the time, it was commonplace for only athletes who raced the individual event at Trials to be considered for relay duty. So, when the Americans took third in the relay, Hall found even more reason to voice his displeasure.

For Thorpe, that first night in Sydney was a glorious evening. He won two of his three gold medals in Sydney, where he finished with five medals overall. It marked the true beginning of his historic legacy, which included gold medals in the 200 and 400 freestyles at the 2004 Olympics. Until Michael Phelps came along, Thorpe was the undisputed king of the sport.

That home Olympiad will forever hold a special place in his heart. "It would have to be the best day of my life, the best hour, the best minute," Thorpe said.

To be able to dream and to fulfill it is the best thing an individual can do. It's amazing to be in this situation and to perform well. I'm one of the select few athletes who have performed at their best at the Olympic Games. The statistics on that are very slim. It's one of the things I wanted to do.

It was pretty amazing in front of my own crowd and it was just fortunate I was able to perform well in front of them. It really was a dream come true. I'm on such a high.

19

Eric the Eel

At the 2000 Olympic Games in Sydney, a swimmer far from medal contention briefly captured the fancy of the sport and the thousands of fans who filled the Sydney Aquatic Centre. He was given a clever nickname by the world's media and has gone down in swimming lore—his story a feel-good tale.

The best 100 freestylers in the world, those who contend for Olympic gold, cover the distance in under 48 seconds. At the time of the 2000 Olympic Games, only one man was in that realm, the Netherlands' Pieter van den Hoogenband. He was the first man to break the 48-second barrier, and he remained alone in that accomplishment for several years.

In his sole Olympic appearance, Eric Moussambani was not close to keeping pace with van den Hoogenband. From Equatorial Guinea, located on the western coast of Middle Africa, Moussambani could not dream of touching the wall in a time anything close to what van den Hoogenband was capable of producing. Really, he was simply hoping to finish his race. It was a pursuit that captured the hearts of the 17,000 spectators at the Sydney Aquatic Centre, instantly made Moussambani a minor celebrity, and earned him a nickname that has become legendary in the sport: "Eric the Eel."

Qualifying for the swimming competition at the Olympic Games varies slightly from country to country. Some nations appoint their teams on the basis of world rankings and previous results, such as those from the World Championships. The world's aquatic superpowers—most notably, the United States and Australia—employ a cutthroat competition in which the difference between elation and heartache can be a hundredth of a second.

At the Olympic Trials of the United States and Australia, only the top two athletes in each event qualify for the Olympic Games. Everyone else goes home. Basically, there are two first-place finishers, with all others the equivalent of last place. An athlete can swim the third-fastest time in the world at the U.S. Trials, good for a bronze medal on the Olympic stage, but if that time is beaten by two countrymen, it's no good.

Moussambani had no qualifying competition to negotiate. As part of a plan by the International Olympic Committee to generate interest in various sports in developing countries, Moussambani was granted a wild card entry to the Sydney Games. Never mind that his country lacked a 50-meter pool, the type used for international competition, and that Moussambani learned to swim a mere 8 months before the start of the 27th Olympiad—in a hotel pool and sometimes a river containing crocodiles, no less. He was in, and he would contest the 100 freestyle (two lengths of the pool), widely considered the premier event of the sport.

When Moussambani arrived in Sydney, he was a complete unknown. He came from a country with no aquatic accolades, one where citizens do not always lead comfortable lives. While Equatorial Guinea boasted the highest per capita wealth of any African country, the majority of its 700,000 residents lived in poverty and under the despotic rule of Teodoro Obiang, whose government was accused of numerous human rights violations, including murder and torture.

In the lead-up to Sydney, Moussambani was greeted with mixed news. He was given the chance to carry his country's flag in the Opening Ceremony, an honor for any athlete. Yet, he learned that he was entered in the 100 freestyle rather than the 50 freestyle, the event that he had prepared to race. Suddenly, the 22-year-old's task was doubly difficult.

When it came time to race, Moussambani, who did not have a coach, looked the part of an Olympic swimmer . . . well, in some ways. Physically, he was a muscled athlete with defined arms, sizable pectoral muscles, and six-pack abdominals. But in a lily-white sport in which color has been and continues to be rare, Moussambani stood out, too, for his skin tone.

He was supposed to race alongside two other swimmers in the first heat of the 100 freestyle, Niger's Karim Bare and Tajikistan's Farkhod Oripov. But Bare and Oripov false-started by significant margins, prompting their disqualification from the event. A quizzical look stretched across Moussambani's face after the disqualifications, as if to ask, "Am I going to swim alone?" Yes, he was. It would be Moussambani against the clock . . . in front of 17,000 fans in a swim-crazed country.

Moussambani dove in after hearing the starting signal and almost immediately had the spectators behind him. Although his physique could pass for that of an internationally acclaimed swimmer, his form could not. He flailed his arms and kicked sporadically, none of the motions in sync. Instead of employing a to-the-side breathing technique, "Eric the Eel" kept his head out of the water for the majority of the race.

There were a few highlights from the first of his two laps. Not only did Moussambani maintain a steady pace for the opening 50 meters, but he also managed to execute a flip turn at the midway point. It wasn't pretty, but it certainly reflected the work and dedication of Moussambani in his preparation for Sydney. Still, there was concern.

"At the turn, Eric the Eel vanished," wrote Craig Lord, the man who created Moussambani's nickname, in the *Times of London*.

> He was under a long time. A hush descended on the crowd. Eric looked like he was caught in a riptide. Was he facing up or down, and did he know it himself? The sense of relief in the venue was tangible when the man from Molabu surfaced to take a breath.
>
> The largely Australian crowd—nearly every man, woman and child probably capable of swimming faster than Moussambani—warmed to the occasion and lifeguards stood by, poised to plunge in for the rescue.

During the second lap, Moussambani's struggles amplified. Would he finish? Would a lifeguard have to leap into the pool and rescue him from drowning? Would he grab onto one of the lane ropes for support? These were all legitimate questions for a swimmer who was barely moving and was drifting to one side of his lane but who was also supported by nearly every person inside the arena.

"This guy doesn't look like he's going to make it," said Adrian Moorhouse, the gold medalist for Great Britain in the 100 breaststroke at the 1988 Olympics in Seoul who was performing commentary for the BBC at the 2000 Games. "I am convinced this guy is going to have to get hold of the lane rope in a moment."

Indeed, Moussambani was within inches of the lane line during the latter stages of his race, but he refused to seek its assistance. Instead, he rallied to move his arms a few more times, eventually touching the wall in a time of 1:52.72, the slowest ever in the event at the Olympics. Credited as the winner of his heat, Moussambani held onto the wall after finishing and drew a few deep breaths—in both exhaustion and relief.

How slow was his time? He was more than a minute behind the winning mark of van den Hoogenband and 50 seconds slower than Bahrain's Dawood Youssef Mohamed Jassim, who finished one place ahead of Moussambani. More, the finalists in the 200 freestyle, held earlier in the meet, each had faster times than Moussambani's effort in the 100 freestyle. The official records of the Olympic Games have Moussambani finishing 71st in the event.

"The first 50 meters were OK, but in the second 50 meters I got a bit worried and thought I wasn't going to make it," Moussambani said immediately after his race. "Then something happened. I think it was all the people getting behind me. I was really, really proud. It's still a great feeling for me and I loved when everyone applauded me at the end. I felt like I had won a medal or something."

Moussambani actually had a female counterpart in Sydney, as he was joined on the Equatorial Guinea team by Paula Barila Bolopa. Unlike her countryman, Bolopa had to swim only 50 meters. Like her teammate, she set a record for time futility while having the crowd behind her every stroke.

Bolopa covered her one lap in 1:03.97, which placed her 73rd and last of the athletes who contested the event. The 72nd-place finisher, Guinea's Aissatou Barry, was timed in 35.79, more than 28 seconds faster. Bolopa, too, was given a nickname before leaving Sydney: "Paula the Crawler."

Of course, there was no medal draped around Moussambani's neck, but he was treated as a celebrity for his heroic swim. He was one of the most popular athletes in the Olympic Village and viewed by some as the definition of the Olympic movement. The founder of the International Olympic Committee and father of the Modern Olympic Games, Frenchman Baron Pierre de Coubertin once said, "The most important thing in the Olympic Games is not winning, but taking the part. The essential thing in life is not conquering, but fighting well." The description fit Moussambani perfectly.

Moussambani had the chance to shake hands with Australia's Michael Klim, his swimming hero. Ian Thorpe, the world's most popular swimmer at the time, offered his approval, saying, "This is what the Olympics is all about." Thorpe's vantage point, though, was not shared by Jacques Rogge, the president of the International Olympic Committee and former Olympian in sailing. Rogge thought that the spectacle was a sham.

Speedo, looking to capitalize on his rising popularity, had Moussambani perform promotional work throughout Europe for the next year. Eventually, that partnership ended, and Moussambani drifted into the shadows. Having improved by a full minute since Sydney, he had hopes of competing at the 2004 Olympic Games in Athens. But errors in his accreditation—likely triggered by the Equatorial Guinea government—prevented that opportunity from developing.

These days, Moussambani serves as the national team coach for Equatorial Guinea, training athletes a few days each week after fulfilling his regular job as an IT engineer. He says that he has improved his career-best time in the 100 free to 55 seconds and is hopeful that he will make an Olympic return at the 2016 Games in Rio de Janeiro. If not, he'll always have Sydney and just under 2 minutes in the Olympic spotlight.

"I have never been so tired in my life," he said in Sydney. "My muscles were hurting. I had never been in a pool that big before. I was very scared. I feel as if I have won a gold medal. Everybody was clapping and cheering me. It was just like winning."

20

A Tie between Teammates

At the 2000 Olympic Games, Anthony Ervin defied the notion that sprinters peak later in their career by sharing the gold medal in the 50 freestyle as a mere 19-year-old.

Training together at the Phoenix Swim Club and living as roommates in the Olympic Village, veteran Gary Hall Jr. and upstart Anthony Ervin wrote an intriguing chapter in the history of sprinting when they shared the gold medal in the 50 freestyle at the 2000 Olympics in Sydney.

Because Gary Hall Jr. saw him every day, was fully aware of his talent level, and knew that he was capable of beating anyone in the world, the veteran Olympian and sprint champion had plenty of respect for what Anthony Ervin brought to the starting blocks.

Because Anthony Ervin saw him every day, was fully aware of his yearning desire, and knew that he wanted individual Olympic gold more than anything else that the sport could provide, the upstart sprinter had plenty of respect for what Gary Hall Jr. brought to the water.

Together, Hall and Ervin wrote one of the most intriguing chapters in Olympic history, when they tied for the gold medal in the 50 freestyle—the one-lap dash that determines the fastest man in water—at the 2000 Olympics in Sydney. The way that they arrived at that point, however, was quite different and only added a level of depth to their tale.

As the 2000 U.S. Olympic Trials in Indianapolis approached, Hall was the best-known name of those contending for a berth on the American squad. Deeply talented, he was a star at the 1996 Olympics in Atlanta, where he anchored the United States to gold medals in the 400 freestyle relay and 400 medley relay and won silver medals in the 50 and 100 freestyles behind Russian sprint legend Alexander Popov.

More, Hall hailed from a family with a rich swimming tradition. His grandfather, Charles Keating Jr., was an NCAA champion for the University of Cincinnati in the 1940s and his uncle, Charles Keating III, a 1976 Olympian. It was Hall's father, though, who had the greatest success in the pool until his son came along.

A three-time Olympian in 1968, 1972, and 1976, Gary Hall Sr. won a medal at each of his three Olympiads, claiming silver in the 400 individual medley in Mexico City (1968), silver in the 200 butterfly in Munich (1972), and bronze in the 100 butterfly in Montreal (1976). His career was also defined by multiple national championships and world records in the 200 butterfly and 200 and 400 individual medleys.

Hall Jr., although a sprinter, simply continued the family tradition. As he made his way up the ranks, Hall was one of the most outspoken voices in the sport. He was not afraid to raise concerns over performance-enhancing drug use, and he possessed a deep confidence that was viewed by some as showboating—namely, his shadow-boxing routine behind the blocks prior to races. More than anything, Hall was letting his personality shine.

In 1999, though, Hall's serious side came to the forefront. Following an incident in which he collapsed, Hall was diagnosed with type 1 diabetes, and doctors initially informed Hall that the diagnosis would put an end to his athletic career. Not satisfied with that outcome, Hall vowed to fight through his disease, and he managed to control his illness with proper attention and care.

As important, Hall became a visible figure in the fight against diabetes, regularly speaking about the positive and active lifestyle that can be enjoyed by those afflicted. He also took part in fund-raising events and activities that gathered money toward research and diabetes care.

"The diabetes was really a major factor in my life, not just my swimming career," said Hall, who was initially scared by the possible effects of diabetes, such as blindness or kidney failure.

The travel took something out of me. It affected my blood sugar levels. But I paid attention to what I ate and made sure I got the right amount of insulin. It was so scary when I was diagnosed. I heard these horror stories and the statistics. My reaction was it's just a matter of time. I've only got so much time before these things happen.

But the quality of life a person with diabetes can have really comes down to the individual and the management that individual can provide. Other people have been able to successfully manage this disease and avoid very serious complications that stem from this disease, so it can be done. If there are complications, it's difficult to blame anybody but yourself.

While Hall was a well-established veteran, Ervin was a soaring youngster, with the Sydney Games on the horizon. One of the nation's top recruits coming out of high school, Ervin wasted little time making an impact upon his emergence at the University of California–Berkeley. During his freshman season, Ervin captured NCAA championships in the 50 and 100 freestyles, victories that quickly turned heads considering his precocious nature. Suddenly, Ervin was a legitimate contender to qualify for the U.S. squad bound for Sydney.

As much as Ervin's talent captured the attention of the media, so did his upbringing. Born to an African American father and Jewish mother, Ervin's biracial background received headlines, primarily because the United States had never had an Olympic swimming medalist with black heritage. For his part, the introspective Ervin tried to shy away from that categorization.

"I have always been proud of my heritage," he said. "But I don't think of it in terms of first of this, first of that. It is like people are trying to pin it down to one definitive thing. I never thought about it. In the nature of American society today, I would think having diverse blood would not be a big deal."

Although their paths to Sydney were different through the end of Ervin's freshman year at Cal, Hall and Ervin came together in Phoenix, Arizona, several months before the U.S. Olympic Trials. At the Phoenix Swim Club, sprint guru Mike Bottom—an assistant coach at Cal at the time—oversaw a talented collection of athletes, headlined by Hall, Ervin, and Poland's Bart Kizierowski, a world-class sprinter in his own right.

Training next to each other, Hall and Ervin now were following a similar blueprint. They took part in identical practices, constantly battled to get to the wall first, and ate the same meals at the same restaurants. Aside from sharing Bottom as a coach, they also shared a sports psychologist and strength trainer.

The fact that Hall and Ervin trained together in pursuit of the same goal and did so while maintaining and further developing a friendship was not exactly the norm. While the Hall-Ervin combination worked in Phoenix, legendary coach Richard Quick was forced to alter his training approach in Northern California. With Jenny Thompson and Dara Torres both under Quick's guidance, the Stanford coach had to separate the athletes because of rising tension and an ultracompetitive atmosphere that was not beneficial to anyone involved.

Clearly, Bottom had a knack for handling the situation with aplomb, while Hall and Ervin possessed the necessary maturity to thrive in such an atmosphere. "Anthony's talent was apparent from day one," Hall said.

> I knew he was a real threat for the gold, and [I] predicted great accomplishments very early on, when he was unproven. I knew that it wasn't going to be easy to beat him, increasingly cognizant of it as the season progressed. At the time, he did not comprehend or appreciate his talent, or the significance of the Olympic Games, which made him even more dangerous as a competitor.
>
> Still, I wanted to help him, and did. He helped me, too. Training with each other elevated both of us. Under the guidance of Mike Bottom [a brilliant psychologist], Anthony and I bought in to a philosophy that all of us had something to contribute and that all ships would rise with the sum contribution.

The approach by Bottom was largely successful because of the way that his athletes bought into his system. Although there was plenty of focus on sprint work in the pool, Bottom was an outside-the-box thinker who engaged his athletes in obstacle course training and other approaches that broke up the monotony of lap after lap in the pool.

The varied coaching style of Bottom is not one that has caught on worldwide, but it has been highly successful. All one has to do is look at the success of his swimmers—most recently, those he coaches as the head man at the University of Michigan. In 2013, Bottom led the Wolverines to the NCAA team title, the program's first since 1995. "My goal was to change the way the world trains sprinters," Bottom said. "I hate to characterize sprinters as a different animal, but they are a different animal. Most coaches end up trying to fit a square peg into a round hole, and we lose a lot of our sprinters."

Leaving Phoenix for the venerable Indianapolis University Natatorium and the Olympic Trials, Hall and Ervin were confident in their chances to nail down berths to Sydney. Indeed, they flourished. Hall led all three rounds of qualifying, while Ervin was third after the preliminaries, then moved into the second position in the semifinals and final.

In the championship final and with invitations to Sydney on the line, both Hall and Ervin broke the 10-year-old American record of Tom Jager, which had stood at 21.81. Hall touched the wall in 21.76, while Ervin wasn't far behind in 21.80. The finish also enhanced the possibility of two Olympic medals in the event.

Along with training partner Anthony Ervin, Gary Hall Jr. shared the gold medal in the 50 freestyle at the 2000 Olympics in Sydney.

For good measure, Hall qualified individually for the 100 freestyle, thanks to a second-place finish, while Ervin's fifth-place finish in the event landed him a berth on the American 400 freestyle relay. Still, the week in Indianapolis wasn't void of a hiccup. After months of dueling in practice and chasing the same goals, Hall and Ervin got into a small spat.

"There was an uncomfortable flair-up at the Olympic Trials," Hall said. "It was basically a brief snarling thing where we growled at each other. I forget what exactly it was over. I immediately wrote it off as the tensions of Trials. We both got over it immediately. Other than that one inconsequential exchange, I have always gotten on well with Anthony."

Bound for Sydney, Hall and Ervin remained tight. At Hall's request, he and Ervin were roommates in the Olympic Village, sharing a four-person suite with Chad Carvin and Ed Moses. The friendship that they had forged in Phoenix only continued to grow, with both men getting a better feel for the other. "Gary is very misunderstood," Ervin said. "Until I roomed with him at the Olympics, I had never really gotten a true glimpse of what Gary is like. He's very deep, and well spoken. We're similar in a lot of ways."

Before they dueled in the 50 freestyle, which is contested in the second half of the Olympic program, Hall and Ervin had the chance to join forces for the United States in the 400 freestyle relay. Despite teaming with Jason Lezak and Neil Walker to post a time under the previous world record, Hall and Ervin could not lift the United States ahead of Australia, which used a sterling leadoff leg from Michael Klim to become the first country other than the United States to win the gold medal in the 400 freestyle relay at the Olympics.

It was a tough blow to take, especially considering the Americans' legacy in the event, but the setback did not floor Hall or Ervin. Before the 50 freestyle, Hall rebounded to claim the bronze medal in the 100 freestyle. The 50 free, though, was the showcase event for Hall and Ervin, and it was an event stacked with talent.

Aside from the American entrants, Popov was the two-time defending world champion and had set a world record just a few months prior to the Sydney Games. Meanwhile, the Netherlands' Pieter van den Hoogenband was riding a hot streak, having already won Olympic gold and set world records in Sydney in the 100 and 200 freestyles. Kizierowski, too, was a factor and a fellow beneficiary of Bottom's training program.

"The coolest thing about Mike is he's not afraid to be nontraditional as a coach," Ervin said before the 2000 Games.

> In some ways, I look at him more on a friendship level than the authoritarian coach. He does tell us what to do, but he gets on a personal level with each of us. If I don't feel like doing something, he'll say, "Let's do something else. What do you want to work on?" So you still get the work done, but your input matters and Mike works with you.

Hall and Ervin moved through the preliminaries as the second- and fourth-fastest qualifiers, with Kizierowski leading the field. In the semifinal round, Hall topped Ervin in the first heat, with van den Hoogenband prevailing in the second semifinal, ahead of Popov. It all set the stage for the final.

The middle of the pool was the focal point, with Hall in lane 4, flanked by Ervin and van den Hoogenband. The mad dash over one length of the pool typically brings paper-thin finishes, but what the athletes saw when they touched the wall was a rarity. Hall and Ervin each stopped the clock in 21.98, followed by van den Hoogenband for the bronze in 22.03. Popov finished a surprising sixth, well back in 22.24.

The tie marked the second time in Olympic history in which the gold medal was shared, joining the 1984 final of the women's 100 freestyle, which saw Americans

Nancy Hogshead and Carrie Steinseifer post identical marks. For Hall and Ervin, digesting the result was not immediate.

"Upon finishing the race, I immediately looked for the place next to my name," Hall said.

> I didn't even look or care for the time. I saw the No. 1 next to my name and started celebrating. Then I noticed that my celebration was sedate compared to my teammate's in the next lane. Happy for him, I looked back at the scoreboard to see a "1" next to his name. I thought "DQ" before I thought "tie." A moment of panic. It felt like a very long time before it became absolutely clear to me what happened. A tie. Then, I couldn't have been happier.

Following Sydney, Hall and Ervin went divergent ways. Never one to focus on the World Championships, Hall dropped off the international scene until it was time to flip the switch for the 2004 Games in Athens and a defense of his Olympic crown. Qualifying for the final with the fifth-fastest time, Hall delivered his finest performance while under pressure, repeating as Olympic champion in 21.93, .01 ahead of Croatia's Duje Draganja, a training partner of Hall who was also mentored by Bottom.

Hall again disappeared after Athens, only to emerge in time for the U.S. Trials for the 2008 Olympics in Beijing. This time, Hall could not spin his magic, and he failed to qualify for his fourth Olympic team. He retired thereafter as a 10-time Olympic medalist.

As for Ervin, his career seemed to be taking off in Sydney, and it continued its upward trajectory at the 2001 World Championships in Fukuoka, Japan, where Ervin was the gold medalist in the 50 and 100 freestyles. Two years later, however, Ervin failed to advance out of the preliminaries of the 50 freestyle at the World Champs, and he followed by walking away from the sport as a 22-year-old.

A free spirit, Ervin spent years uninvolved with swimming at a competitive level, although he gave lessons to help pay the rent. He bounced around the country, played guitar in a band, and even auctioned off his gold medal from the 2000 Olympics, with the proceeds going to victims of the 2004 Indian Ocean tsunami.

As his 30th birthday neared, he got back into training after an 8-year layoff. The results that followed were almost unfathomable. Ervin, long touted as a naturally gifted sprinter, proved to be faster than ever and qualified for the 2012 Olympic Games in London, where he finished fifth. A year later, he helped the United States to a silver medal at the World Championships in the 400 freestyle relay and placed sixth in the 50 freestyle, although he set a personal-best time in the semifinals.

Many experts believe that Ervin could have become one of the greatest sprinters in history, ranking alongside Popov. But Ervin isn't into regret and looks at the road that he traveled in matter-of-fact style. "I really felt like I had accomplished every goal I had set out to," Ervin said.

> It became time to go back and reclaim some of the stuff I had sacrificed along the way. I was kind of shot down this tunnel. As a youth, as most people are, you're not really given

a ton of options for a variety of reasons. When something sticks, people often stay with it. For whatever reason, I couldn't do that. I was convinced the grass would be greener somewhere else. Or, at the least, if I did make the journey that I would see the other side of that horizon, whatever was there. I think everybody's got that to a certain degree. But I certainly had a lot of angst and resistance toward being pushed in the direction I had always been going. I really just needed freedom, so I took it.

Undoubtedly, Hall and Ervin did things their way and boasted opposing tales. One was the veteran champion, the other the rising star. Hall possessed a passion for his sport and placed his focus almost entirely on one competition: the Olympic Games. Ervin, meanwhile, was content to leave the competition pool behind and explore other aspects of life. But when their names are mentioned, one day immediately comes to mind—that moment on September 22, 2000, when Hall and Ervin, friends and training partners, stood together on the medals podium as Olympic champions.

"I don't mind sharing the gold medal podium," Hall said. "It couldn't have happened to a nicer guy, a guy I practice with all the time. It was like another day of practice."

Albeit with a lot more on the line.

21

Race of the Century

At the 2004 Olympic Games in Athens, Michael Phelps decided to clash with Ian Thorpe and Pieter van den Hoogenband in a race that went down in history.

The 200 freestyle had enough substance at the 2004 Olympics, thanks to a repeat clash between the Netherlands' Pieter van den Hoogenband and Australia's Ian Thorpe. But when Michael Phelps entered the fray, too, the race became something special and one of the most anticipated events in Olympic history.

How many times has this refrain been uttered by sports fans and experts? "Wouldn't it be great if (fill in the blank) and (fill in the blank) had the chance to battle?" In many instances, the desired matchup is left only to the imagination, with timing usually the most significant factor in the blockage of what could be an epic duel.

As the 2004 Olympic Games neared, however, swimming found itself in a fortunate position when three of the biggest names of the era—or history, for that matter—decided that the 200 freestyle was going to be on their Athens schedules. The revelation had the sport's analysts wringing their hands and fans counting down to what undoubtedly would be a day to remember: August 16, 2004.

Two of the pieces for an epic race in Athens were in place long before the Games returned to their birthplace. In Australian Ian Thorpe and Dutchman Pieter van den Hoogenband, the 200 freestyle featured two of the greatest performers the event had seen. From 1999 to 2001, Thorpe and van den Hoogenband combined to set eight world records in the event, with Thorpe leading the way with six global standards. The men had also met 4 years earlier in a splendid showdown at the 2000 Olympics in Sydney, so Athens was a part II of sorts, a second chapter that carried little risk of failing to match up to the first clash.

The event, though, surged even greater in expectations when Michael Phelps—never one to shy away from a challenge—announced that he was going to give the four-lap discipline a go. It would be one of five individual events and eight overall for Phelps, who was in pursuit of matching (or eclipsing) the seven gold medals won by Mark Spitz at the 1972 Olympics in Munich.

In his other individual events—the 100 and 200 butterflies and the 200 and 400 individual medleys—Phelps was a favorite to walk away with a gold medal. The 200 freestyle was a different story, with the sport's rising star playing the role of underdog in what only added to the intrigue of the event. But for Phelps and coach Bob Bowman, the opportunity to race against the best was too alluring. "This is the best opportunity for me to swim in the fastest 200 [freestyle] in history," Phelps said ahead of Athens. "I love a challenge."

To gain a full appreciation for what unfolded in Athens, it is necessary to examine the years leading up to the Olympiad, particularly what unfolded in Sydney in 2000. At the time, Thorpe and van den Hoogenband were already stars, each etching his own legacy in Olympic lore—and doing so with the help of the other.

Racing in front of a home crowd, which topped out at 17,000 spectators, a 17-year-old Thorpe was sensational in his Olympic debut, winning the 400 freestyle in a world-record time. Since winning his first world title in the event at the age of 15, Thorpe was deemed a future star, so talented that he could go down as the best swimmer that the sport had ever seen.

With the 400 freestyle title in his pocket, Thorpe figured to win the 200 freestyle, too. One problem: van den Hoogenband had a different plan. The bronze medalist in the 200 freestyle at the 1998 World Championships, van den Hoogenband had developed into one of the world's elite 100 and 200 freestylers. If there was some-one who could derail Thorpe and do it on the Aussie's home turf, it was the Flying Dutchman. That possibility became even more evident when van den Hoogenband sent a statement in the semifinals in Sydney, producing a world record of 1:45.35. Although Thorpe won the other semifinal in 1:45.37, there was no longer any belief that the final would be a coronation for the Aussie.

The final in Sydney played out as expected in the early stages, with van den Hoogenband surging to the front of the field and forcing Thorpe to run him down over the final lap. But as the swimmers covered the final meters, Thorpe could not overcome his rival, and he watched van den Hoogenband equal his world record from the semifinals. A stunned Australian crowd could do nothing more than ap-preciate what "Hoogie" had done: slay the dragon in his own lair. "It was amazing to do this," van den Hoogenband said. "In his home nation, in his home city, in his home pool. It was so eerie. [With] 25 meters left, I didn't see him creeping up on me. I thought, 'Man, he's not going to touch me.'"

Thorpe finished his home Olympiad with five medals, three gold and two silver, while van den Hoogenband added a gold medal and world record in the 100 freestyle to go with bronze medals in the 50 freestyle and as a member of the Dutch 800 free-style relay. While Thorpe and van den Hoogenband were constantly in the spotlight, Phelps flew under the radar—the last such time in his career. A month earlier at the U.S. Olympic Trials, a furious finish by the 15-year-old in the 200 butterfly landed Phelps his first Olympic invitation. His accomplishment made him the youngest male Olympian for the United States in swimming in 68 years.

Although Bowman and higher-ups with USA Swimming knew the future for Phelps had no ceiling, he certainly was not the talk of the American team. Sure, jour-nalist Paul McMullen of the *Baltimore Sun* followed Phelps's moves closely, providing strong reporting to those from Phelps's hometown. But on the bigger stage, Phelps was a role player on a U.S. team that featured established stars such as Gary Hall Jr., Lenny Krayzelburg, Jenny Thompson, and Dara Torres.

Phelps had just one event to contest in Sydney and had no trouble handling the pres-sure that would floor many other teenagers competing on the biggest stage in athletics. Phelps went through the preliminaries of the 200 fly as the third-fastest qualifier, then moved through the semifinals with the fourth-fastest time. It was becoming clear that Phelps—although maybe not in Sydney—was not going to be denied much longer.

In the final, Phelps used his customary late charge to put himself in medal con-tention, but the wall crept up a shade too early, as he finished fifth in 1:56.50, 33 hundredths shy of the bronze medal–winning time posted by Australian Justin Nor-ris. In the six races that he contested at the Olympic Trials and Olympic Games, Phelps established a personal best in each. One day, it was surmised, there would be no stopping a guy who had all the right tools.

"How do you stand this?" legendary coach Mark Schubert asked Bowman in Sydney. "I have never seen anyone his age like him. You look at the Olympic Trials, the most pressure-packed meet in the world, and now the Olympics. He is truly phenomenal."

Over the next few years, Thorpe and van den Hoogenband continued to excel, with Thorpe besting his foe for world titles in the 200 freestyle in 2001 and 2003. Thorpe was at his best at the 2001 World Championships, where he won six gold medals and set world records in the 200, 400, and 800 freestyles. Van den Hoogenband was a constant force as well, and while he finished short of any world championships, he was a regular presence on the podium.

What changed the most was the profile of Phelps, who in short fashion soared from rising star to one of the world's elite performers. By 2001, he was a world-record holder and world champion and, by the close of the 2003 World Championships, an all-around stud—the best that the globe had to offer in the 200 butterfly and 200 and 400 individual medleys. He was also right there in the 100 butterfly, trailing only American teammate Ian Crocker for world supremacy.

At those 2003 World Championships, Phelps and Thorpe locked up in the 200 individual medley, hardly a strong event for the Aussie. Ultimately, Phelps prevailed by more than 3 seconds over Thorpe, the silver medalist. As a result of that head-to-head triumph by Phelps and the overall depth of his program, it was argued that Phelps had moved ahead of Thorpe as the sport's Poseidon. Still, the freestyle was Thorpe's domain, and Phelps—outside of duty in the 800 freestyle relay—had not ventured into that territory. Of course, that scenario soon changed.

In the months leading up to the 2004 U.S. Olympic Trials in Long Beach, California, there was a great deal of speculation concerning Phelps's program for the Athens Games. Because Phelps and Bowman kept their plans a well-guarded secret, all that was known was that Phelps would embrace a multievent slate. Eventually, it was revealed that the 200 freestyle would be part of the agenda, thus enhancing the hype concerning the event come Athens.

With Thorpe, van den Hoogenband, and Phelps all targeting the event, the 200 freestyle had it all: The world-record holder and two-time defending world champion. The reigning Olympic champion and former world-record holder. The upstart. It was soap opera stuff, played out across three continents.

"I don't see us as being animals and marking our territory," Thorpe said.

> Not yet. I don't think there's anyone's territory. I enjoy challenging myself rather than it just being about who's in the race. I think Michael wanted to swim this race not just because I was in it, but you know, I think he wanted another challenge. For athletes, that's what we're here to do. I'm glad that I've had the opportunity to race against some of the world's best athletes in my event.

Looking for a way to add excitement to the event (not that it was needed), the press dubbed the impending showdown among Thorpe, van den Hoogenband, and Phelps as the Race of the Century. Really, it was a fitting title considering the credentials of those involved.

Unlike 4 years earlier, when van den Hoogenband blasted a world record before the final, the combatants advanced through the opening two rounds in measured fashion. Van den Hoogenband won the first semifinal, while Thorpe finished ahead of Phelps in the second semifinal, with all three men saving their best for when it mattered most.

When the final under the Athens sky unfolded, intrigue was certainly in the air. Thorpe and van den Hoogenband were considered the favorites, but a persistent question was on the lips of those in attendance: can Phelps make this a three-man battle for gold? The answer proved to be a negative, but it did nothing to take the shine off the Race of the Century.

At the 50-meter mark, van den Hoogenband was out in front, with Thorpe sitting just off the pace in second and Phelps in fourth. As the swimmers hit the midway point, van den Hoogenband had increased his lead over Thorpe, 50.42 to 51.04, with Phelps now sitting third in 51.70. That is when Thorpe started to reel in van den Hoogenband.

Unable to play catch-up in Sydney 4 years earlier, Thorpe cut into van den Hoogenband's lead on the third lap and overtook the Dutchman on the final lap to prevail in 1:44.71, with van den Hoogenband earning the silver medal in 1:45.23. Producing the fastest last-lap split, Phelps touched in an American record of 1:45.32 for the bronze medal.

"It was the final that excited a lot of people," Thorpe said.

This has been played out on three continents in the leadup to the Olympic Games, so it became a big deal. But I wasn't focused on that. I really wanted to concentrate on what I was trying to do, make sure I swam the race well. I was able to do that. For me, that's how I approached my races and I have been able to be successful in the past. I don't worry about what my competitors are doing. I said to [van den Hoogenband], "Well, I guess that makes it 1–1 and I'd like to see you again in Beijing."

That brings up the question that was asked before, and you know I intend to be swimming it again. Pieter and I are good friends and it is a wonderful experience to be able to challenge yourself in this race, to prepare so hard in it. And you know, that's what I've done, and that's what Pieter's done. And Michael's done exactly the same thing. It's good to be able to go out there and experience that with people that you know well. People kind of have their fate and their destiny and that was what it was tonight. I've worked damn hard for this.

With the United States taking the bronze medal in the 400 freestyle relay earlier in the competition and Phelps winning the bronze medal in the 200 freestyle, his pursuit of Spitz's seven gold medals from Munich was over. Some members of the media called Phelps's performance in Athens a disappointment, but his eight medals told another story.

By winning both butterfly events and both individual medley disciplines to go with a pair of relay gold medals, Phelps surpassed Spitz's overall medal haul. Making the effort more impressive was the fact that Phelps, thanks to the sport's global

growth, faced deeper competition than Spitz and had handled a schedule that included semifinal rounds, something that Spitz did not have to negotiate in events
200 meters and longer.

"How can I be disappointed?" Phelps asked after the 200 freestyle.

I swam in a field with the two fastest freestylers of all time and I was right there with
them. I'm extremely happy with that. It's a [personal] best time. It's a new American
record. I wanted to race those guys and that's what I did. It was fun.

It's a lot more emotionally draining than anything I have done before and it takes
a lot out of you race to race, particularly tonight. When those guys are going so fast it
makes it real exciting, but it's tough. I had an opportunity and I tried to do something
that [Spitz] did, but I didn't. When I started to swim, I never thought I would have an
opportunity to go for seven.

The summit meeting that took place in Athens figured to be followed up at some
point. Instead, it marked the final time that Thorpe, van den Hoogenband, and
Phelps raced against one another. Thorpe initially announced that he was taking a
break from competition following the 2004 Games, but he never raced internationally again. Ahead of the 2012 Olympics, Thorpe announced a comeback attempt
that blew up, with the middle-distance legend far from qualifying for the Australian
squad that competed at the London Games.

Van den Hoogenband and Phelps met again in the 200 freestyle at the 2007
World Championships, and the outcome was a one-sided affair, with Phelps taking
down Thorpe's 5-year-old world record with a time of 1:43.86 and with van den
Hoogenband settling for the silver medal in another zip code, 1:46.28.

The dominance of Phelps, who won seven gold medals at the 2007 World
Champs, could only be appreciated by van den Hoogenband, who announced after
the final in Melbourne that he would abandon the 200 freestyle going forward,
choosing instead to focus his energy on the 100 freestyle, where he was the two-time
defending champion.

"I was swimming OK," van den Hoogenband said. "But after every turn, he was
pushing off and kicking through the water extremely fast. I was like, 'Let's see what
he's got left for the last 50.' Well, he had a lot left. I thought the 200 freestyle record
by [Thorpe] would last for 10, maybe 20 years."

At the 2008 Olympics in Beijing, where Phelps surpassed Spitz with an iconic
eight-for-eight gold medal performance, Phelps obliterated the opposition in the
200 freestyle, taking his world record down to 1:42.96. That time proved to be
more than a second faster than anything that Thorpe or van den Hoogenband ever
produced. For his part, van den Hoogenband was fifth in the 100 freestyle in Beijing
but became the first man to make the final of the 100 freestyle in four consecutive
Olympiads. Aside from his two victories, he was fourth as an 18-year-old in 1996.

All told, the Race of the Century brought together three men who combined for
38 Olympic medals, 22 by Phelps. In a little less than 2 minutes, Thorpe, van den
Hoogenband, and Phelps showed the beauty of what can happen when three legends

get together. They thrilled a fan base. They brought something to the sport that will never be forgotten.

TABLE 21.1

The Race of the Century was the name given to the 2004 Athens Olympics show-down among Australian Ian Thorpe, the Netherlands' Pieter van den Hoogenband, and the United States' Michael Phelps in the 200 freestyle. Thorpe came out with the gold medal in a race that matched three of the greatest male swimmers in history. Here's a look at how the race unfolded.

Athlete	50 M	100 M	150 M	Finish
Ian Thorpe	24.81	51.04	1:17.92	1:44.71
Pieter van den Hoogenband	24.44	50.42	1:17.72	1:45.23
Michael Phelps	25.22	51.70	1:18.83	1:45.32

GRAPH 21.1

The Race of the Century was so loaded with talent that the three main combatants—Ian Thorpe, Pieter van den Hoogenband, and Michael Phelps—combined for 38 medals during their Olympic careers. Here's a look at their individual medal breakdowns.

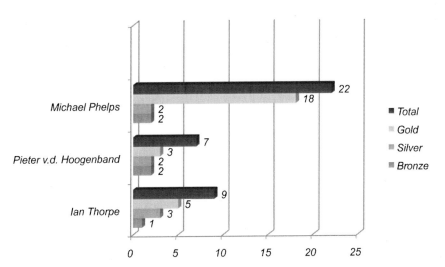

22

An Illegal Kickstart

Although Kosuke Kitajima got the best of him at the Olympic Games, Brendan Hansen put together a storied career with several world championships and world records in the breaststroke events.

The final of the 100 breaststroke at the 2004 Olympics in Athens was shrouded in controversy after Japan's Kosuke Kitajima was shown performing an illegal kick on the way to defeating American Brendan Hansen. The move by Kitajima set off a charge of cheating by Hansen's teammate and close friend Aaron Peirsol and proved to be the impetus for a rule change in the stroke.

Certain athletes will be forever linked. While many boast stand-alone credentials of great prestige, some possess a bond with another that is inescapable. On the basketball court, only first names were needed: Larry and Magic. In the ring, it was Ali vs. Frazier. On the grass of Wimbledon, it was Borg vs. McEnroe.

Swimming, too, has had its share of high-profile rivalries, duels spanning all the strokes. In the breaststroke discipline, there has been nothing close to matching the rivalry of the United States' Brendan Hansen and Japan's Kosuke Kitajima. For a little more than a decade, the men pushed each other—and their events—to greater heights. A coolness primarily permeated the relationship, a language barrier not helping matters, although warmth was found when their dueling was done.

For all the showdowns shared between Hansen and Kitajima—from Japan to Spain, Canada, Australia, and beyond—nothing compares to what unfolded in a little more than a minute at the 2004 Olympic Games in Athens. The events of August 15 defined—in part—a pair of careers and ultimately triggered a change to the breaststroke that continues to bring controversy.

The early years of the Hansen-Kitajima rivalry resembled a tennis match, with the men volleying accomplishments and titles back and forth. Kitajima broke onto the Olympic stage first, qualifying to race the 100 and 200 breaststrokes at the 2000 Games in Sydney. Although Kitajima failed to advance beyond the preliminaries of the longer distance, he just missed a medal in the 100 breast, finishing fourth. As important, he gained valuable experience that proved beneficial in the years—and Olympiads—to come.

Hansen, however, experienced his first true heartache during the 2000 campaign. At the U.S. Olympic Trials in Indianapolis, an 18-year-old Hansen placed third in both the 100 and 200 breaststrokes. With only the top-two finishers in each event qualifying for the Olympic Games, Hansen found himself in the worst position possible. The 200 breaststroke was particularly agonizing, as Hansen was charging down the last lap and gaining ground on the leaders with every stroke. Had the race been 201 meters, he probably would have earned a trip to Sydney. Instead, he was 15 hundredths of a second short.

Several athletes in Hansen's position have allowed that near-Olympic miss to mentally destroy them, to cast doubt over whether they could get over the hump and achieve a lifelong dream. Hansen, exhibiting maturity well beyond his teenage years, opted for a different approach. Although deeply disappointed, he used the events in Indianapolis to drive him.

"There were a few days when I didn't see the light at the end of the tunnel. It was hard," he said. "But I'm going to use it as a positive. You can't regret what happened in the past, but you can use it as motivation, for myself and my teammates. I'm a man on a mission."

Off to the storied program at the University of Texas following the Olympic Trials, Hansen did not waste time grinding away under the watch of coach Eddie Reese. During his freshman year, he won the first of four NCAA titles each in the 100 and 200 breaststrokes, with that momentum leading to the biggest moment of his career (to date) at the 2001 World Championships in Fukuoka, Japan. While not considered a favorite, Hansen captured the gold medal with a championship-record time of 2:10.69, with Kitajima picking up the bronze medal a little more than a half second back.

"His swimming at the [Olympic] Trials was a great indicator of his ability," Reese said of Hansen. "To get third in both events would floor most people. Not Brendan. He took no time to get back on his horse and get back to work."

The battle between Hansen and Kitajima was clearly on. They each walked away with one individual title at the 2002 Pan Pacific Championships, but the end of that season and the 2003 campaign belonged to Kitajima. He set his first world record in the 200 breaststroke at the end of 2002, breaking the iconic 10-year-old standard of American Mike Barrowman. Then at the 2003 World Championships, Kitajima broke world records en route to gold medals in both the 100 and 200 breaststrokes, with Hansen taking silver and bronze, respectively.

It didn't take long, however, for the momentum to shift back in Hansen's favor. At the 2004 U.S. Olympic Trials in Long Beach, California, Hansen popped—arguably—the two biggest performances of the meet. He shaved 48 hundredths off Kitajima's world record in the 100 breaststroke and sliced 38 hundredths off Kitajima's global mark in the 200 breaststroke. The stage was set for an epic duel at the 2004 Games in Athens, the birthplace of the Olympics.

Brendan Hansen's career ended with six Olympic medals, including a surprise bronze medal in the 100 breaststroke at the 2012 Games in London.

Neither Hansen nor Kitajima had any difficulty navigating the preliminaries and semifinals of the 100 breaststroke, although their times did not match what they previously produced. Still, as the men took to the blocks for the final of the 100 breast on August 15 (Hansen's birthday), the spectators at the outdoor venue expected a down-to-the-wire duel.

Indeed, a neck-and-neck showdown is what evolved. Stroke for stroke over two laps, Hansen and Kitajima battled. As they touched the wall and looked to the scoreboard, it showed that Kitajima got to the touchpad first, his time of 1:00.08 narrowly edging Hansen's 1:00.25. At the realization of his triumph, Kitajima let out several primal screams, much to the dismay of Hansen. But the screaming was just starting.

Underwater cameras used for television purposes showed that Kitajima twice violated a rule of the stroke. He was shown using a downward dolphin kick at the start of the race and again after the turn at the 50-meter mark. At the time, the event did not allow for any dolphin kicks, unlike the other strokes in the sport.

Hansen didn't cry foul at the end of the race. For one, that wasn't his style. More, he had no way of knowing what transpired in the lane next to him. Hansen was fixated on his race, and that is where he remained after it had concluded. Hansen saw the clock and knew that he was nearly a second slower than the time that he produced at the Olympic Trials. He blamed only himself for not claiming victory.

The inability of Hansen to replicate what he did at Trials was not an unfamiliar scene in American swimming. With only two individuals able to qualify for the Olympics in an individual event, coupled with the vast depth of talent in the United States, there is no margin for error at the Olympic Trials. Athletes must push the pedal to the floor to ensure their Olympic invitation.

This setup, though, has been problematic. With a short turnaround between Trials and the Olympic Games, athletes frequently have not had the necessary time to increase their training and get the proper rest needed to perform at their peak. This was the scenario met by Hansen, and it hurt.

While Hansen was mum on the sight of Kitajima's dolphin kicking on two occasions, his teammates were not prepared to stay quiet. Sprinter Jason Lezak voiced his displeasure over Kitajima's tactics, but his words hardly resonated when juxtaposed with the statements of Aaron Peirsol, Hansen's good friend and teammate at the University of Texas. Peirsol, who swept the backstroke events at the Athens Games, went on the offensive almost immediately after the race.

"He knew what he was doing," Peirsol said. "It's cheating. Something needs to be done about that. It's just ridiculous. You take a huge dolphin kick and that gives you extra momentum, but he knows that you can't see that from underwater. He's got a history of that. Pay attention to it."

Experts in the sport, primarily coaches, figured that the power of a dolphin kick was good for up to two-tenths of a second per lap, meaning that Kitajima's usage easily provided the winning difference over Hansen. But none of the deckside judges saw or were willing to call the violations, and because video replay is not used in

En route to the gold medal in the 100 breaststroke at the 2004 Olympics in Athens, Japan's Kosuke Kitajima was accused of cheating at two different points in his race, allegations which tainted his golden moment.

swimming, technology could not be employed. With no room to file a protest, Hansen was out of luck. He was admirable in the way that he handled the situation.

"It would be a big deal for an official to come out and to disqualify somebody," Hansen said.

> I can only account for my actions and I know exactly what I did in my race. Everything else, I hope the officials who are sitting right next to me will take care of that. They are not there to have a front-row seat and watch the Olympic Games. They're there to take care of the rules. I believe that's what they do.
>
> I don't agree with [Peirsol's] actions because the U.S. is very diplomatic on these sorts if things. He was a little fired up and he was protecting his teammate, that's all.

Kitajima initially declined to address the topic after the race, although his coach, Norimasa Hirai, defended his pupil by indicating he never performed an illegal kick. A day later, with the 200 breaststroke looming, Kitajima discussed the accusations levied by Peirsol and maintained his innocence.

"There's nothing about the race I actually remember," Kitajima said.

I got in and did the best I could. I just remember when I finished and I won, I was as happy as I've ever been. A lot of people will now start to pay attention more than before. When I heard the comments by Peirsol, I was really surprised because I always try to have fair competition. I'm always trying my best within the regulations. I have never, ever been cautioned by the official judges.

Three days after claiming his controversial gold medal in the 100 breaststroke, Kitajima left no doubt about his dominance in the 200 breaststroke, winning by more than a second over Hungarian Daniel Gyurta, with Hansen taking the bronze medal. Hansen got his gold on the final night of action when he joined Peirsol, Ian Crocker, and Lezak on the triumphant 400 medley relay.

The controversy sparked by the final of the 100 breaststroke in Athens did not dissipate, and it forced a rule change to the sport. Almost a year after Kitajima's clouded win, FINA, the international governing body of swimming, decided to amend its regulations by allowing athletes a single dolphin kick off the start of each race and off each turn. Basically, rather than placing the onus on officials to enforce the rules, FINA took the easy way out.

In the meantime, Hansen regained the upper hand in the rivalry with Kitajima. Hansen won gold medals in the 100 and 200 breaststroke events at the 2005 World Championships in Montreal, then won both events at the 2006 Pan Pacific Championships, twice beating Kitajima and lowering the world record in the 200 breaststroke. Before illness forced Hansen to withdrawal from the 200 breaststroke at the 2007 World Championships in Melbourne, he again beat Kitajima in the 100 breast.

The 2008 Olympics, though, proved to be forgettable for the American. Before the Beijing Games, Hansen failed to qualify for the 200 breast, leaving him with just the 100 breaststroke and medley relay on his schedule. Hansen's inability to qualify in the 200 breast elicited a jab from Kitajima, who said, "For a swimmer of his level, it shouldn't be that difficult to qualify. He didn't seem to set his goals and rise to the challenge just one month before the Olympics."

Kitajima went on to repeat his Olympic sweep of the breaststroke events in Beijing, while Hansen finished out of the medals in the 100 breast, placing fourth. Although Hansen helped the United States prevail in the medley relay, it was another bitter Olympic experience. Hansen ultimately retired after the Beijing Games, content to explore other endeavors. Kitajima, meanwhile, took a sabbatical in 2009 before returning to the sport.

Eventually, the competitive urge got the best of Hansen, and he returned to action in time to qualify for the 2012 Olympics in London. With lower expectations than for his previous Olympic experiences, Hansen competed without pressure. He barely squeaked into the final of the 100 breaststroke, grabbing the last spot for the final. But racing out of lane 8, Hansen managed to collect the bronze medal, calling his latest piece of hardware "the shiniest bronze medal ever." He also beat Kitajima in an individual Olympic race for the first time, with Kitajima finishing fifth. The medley relay on the last day of the meet saw Hansen win another gold with Team USA and Kitajima pick up silver with his Japanese teammates.

The final in London, much like Athens, was not without controversy. Underwater video footage showed several swimmers—most notably, South African gold medalist Cameron van der Burgh—performing several dolphin kicks off the start. Shockingly, van der Burgh later admitted to utilizing more than the single dolphin kick allowed by the rule change of 2005. The regulation change that the governing body hoped would eliminate problems a year after Athens still has not proven successful. Additionally, FINA has continually refused the implementation of an underwater-camera review system, much to the chagrin of athletes and coaches.

At the end of their final duel, Hansen and Kitajima put aside the jabs that had been exchanged through the years and paid each other respect through Twitter. They also posed for a picture with each other after a press conference and exchanged a few words. Growing together in the sport clearly generated an appreciation level for each other's talents. "We had a good run against each other," Hansen said.

With one race in Athens serving as a defining moment.

23

An Anchor's Way

Jason Lezak proved heroic as the anchor of the United States' 400 freestyle relay at the 2008 Games in Beijing, and also kept alive Michael Phelps' pursuit of history.

When Jason Lezak entered the water for the United States on the anchor leg of the United States' 400 freestyle relay at the 2008 Olympic Games in Beijing, the race was seemingly over. Lezak trailed Frenchman Alain Bernard by a body length, and overcoming that deficit appeared impossible. But Lezak, behind the greatest anchor leg in history, gradually reeled in Bernard to give the United States an improbable gold medal.

History will remember Jason Lezak as an accomplished sprint freestyler, one of the better produced in those events over the past few decades. He will be remembered as an individual Olympic medalist, a lengthy journey leading the native Southern Californian to that status. He will also be remembered for a shortfall on the Olympic stage—the Athens Games of 2004 hardly memorable.

More than anything, though, Lezak will be remembered for what he managed to accomplish in less than 47 seconds on the morning of August 11, 2008. Putting together what is inarguably the greatest relay performance in the history of the sport, Lezak carried the United States to the gold medal in the 400 freestyle relay. It sounds so simple. It was anything but an easy task.

At the 2000 Olympics in Sydney, Lezak was supposed to be part of a 400 freestyle relay that maintained the United States' legacy in the event. Never before had the United States, the dominant swim nation in the world, lost the event at an Olympic Games in which it competed. It was perfect: seven for seven. Claiming gold medal No. 8 was just a formality, right? Wrong.

Racing against an Australian quartet fueled by 17,000 spectators cheering on the home team, the American streak came to a sudden and jolting halt. As anchormen Ian Thorpe and Gary Hall Jr. approached the wall for the finish, the outcome remained in doubt. But when the final result flashed onto the scoreboard, there it was: gold for Australia, Thorpe having ended the American reign.

Lezak managed a gold medal in Sydney in the 400 medley relay, a reward for swimming the freestyle leg of the U.S. preliminary team. However, Olympic pain again struck 4 years later. Again, Lezak was able to win gold in the 400 medley relay, this time handling the anchor leg for the United States in the championship final. But what preceded that success was difficult to swallow.

Early in the meet, the United States watched its chance of regaining the 400 freestyle relay title die a painful death. A horrid leadoff leg by Ian Crocker buried the United States from the start, and while the middle legs were solid, Lezak was passed in the final meters for the silver medal by the Netherlands' Pieter van den Hoogenband. The United States, in Lezak's two Olympic appearances in the event, had gone from perfect to silver to bronze . . . and the worst was still to come.

Having set the American record in the 100 freestyle at the U.S. Olympic Trials in Long Beach, California, Lezak was among the top medal contenders in Athens. If he couldn't stay with van den Hoogenband—the reigning champion and world-record holder—he surely would get the silver or bronze. Instead, Lezak bombed completely, unable to advance beyond the preliminaries. It was akin to Tiger Woods—at the top of his game—firing rounds of 83 and 84 at the Masters and missing the cut by an abysmal margin.

Lezak had no one to blame but himself. There was no illness to cite nor a botched start or turn. Lezak simply misjudged the swim, thinking that he could ease off the accelerator and still cruise into the semifinal round. If there is a place to not make that kind of error, it's at the Olympic Games.

"I just didn't swim my race smart, and I paid for it," said Lezak, stating the obvious.

By the time that the 2008 Olympics in Beijing were ready to unfold, Lezak had overcome the disappointments of Athens. He finished fourth in the 100 freestyle at the 2005 World Championships and placed fifth in the 100 freestyle at the 2007 World Championships. Along the way, there were additional gold medals in relay duty, including triumphs in the 400 free relay at each of the aforementioned World Champs. In part due to Lezak, the United States was on the cusp of regaining Olympic glory in an event that it once owned.

Despite the United States' recent success in international action, the road to Olympic redemption was not going to be free of obstacles. Looming largely—figuratively and literally—was France. Not only had the French posted impressive times throughout the year, but they also went into the final with what was supposed to be a trump card in anchor Alain Bernard. From a muscular standpoint, Bernard could have doubled for the Incredible Hulk; he was also the world-record holder in the 100 freestyle. If he had the lead going into the final leg, the race was over.

So confident was Bernard that he engaged in some trash-talking in the days leading up to the 400 freestyle relay. Of an impending matchup with the Americans, Bernard didn't mince words.

"The Americans?" Bernard asked rhetorically. "We're going to smash them. That's what we came here for."

Not surprisingly, the French commentary did not sit well in the American camp. The quartet of Michael Phelps, Garrett Weber-Gale, Cullen Jones, and Lezak used the foreign bravado as motivation. For Phelps, it was a common strategy. For years, Phelps used slights—perceived or otherwise—to ignite his competitive fire. Now, he was sharing that tactic with teammates.

The Water Cube—formally, the Beijing Aquatic Center—was electric as the relay finalists were introduced just before the final, and the United States used that energy to bolt to the lead at the midway point. While Phelps led off with an American-record performance, Weber-Gale was equally strong. That tandem provided the United States with a cushion of .43 over France. It was an advantage that quickly disappeared. With Frenchman Frederick Bousquet splitting 46.63 on the third leg to the 47.65 of Jones, France had turned its deficit into a lead of .59. And with Bernard on the end of the French relay, few thought that Lezak would get the job done. That group included Lezak himself. "The thought really entered my mind for a split second," Lezak said. "There's no way."

More than a half second after Bernard entered the water, Lezak flew off the blocks. He flew through the water like he had never done before, producing a superb first lap. But as Bernard and Lezak flipped for the final 50 meters home, Lezak still trailed by a noticeable margin. With 25 meters left, Lezak was still noticeably behind. But that is when the race started to change.

In a tactical error, Bernard was racing on the left side of his lane. That decision was a faulty one, as it allowed Lezak, swimming on the right side of his lane, to get a draft off the Frenchman. With each stroke, Lezak cut into the lead of Bernard, and a slam-dunk victory for France became more and more in doubt. Dan Hicks and

Finishing No. 1 became a trademark for Michael Phelps, whose knack for delivering under pressure was one of the defining characteristics of his career.

Rowdy Gaines, the NBC duo calling the swimming action, had to reverse field on their call that Lezak simply could not pull off such a huge comeback. Then again, no one in the venue thought that Lezak could track down Bernard. Well . . .

"I was just thinking to myself, if there's anyone on this team or in the world that is going to do it, it was going to be Jason," Weber-Gale said.

With a few meters to go, it still appeared that France would earn the gold medal. But as Bernard and Lezak lunged for the wall and stretched their arms out to activate the touchpad, it was Lezak who got there first. Thanks to an epic anchor leg—officially in the books at 46.06—the United States prevailed by eight hundredths of a second. The American team erupted—both the relay that won and the teammates in the athletes' section of the stands. Phelps flexed on deck, hugs were shared, and Lezak was fondly patted on the head. In the adjacent lane, Bernard was crestfallen.

No one had ever come close to splitting 46.06 before, and Lezak needed every bit of that swim to send the Americans to the top step of the medals podium. In the United States, where swimming is generally an afterthought on the sporting landscape, the victory became one of the biggest stories of the day. It was only the second final of eight for Phelps during his quest to break Mark Spitz's record of seven gold medals in a single Olympiad, but it turned out to be a major moment in Phelps's history-making week.

"It would have to be in the unbelievable category," said U.S. head coach Eddie Reese, regarded as one of the world's best in his profession.

That's the biggest word I know. It had to be the best ever and it was the best ever. That's the kind of anchor you dream of. When you put the world-record holder in on the end of a relay and you go into the pool behind him, the chance of you beating him is slim and none. There's never been [something like that] in my memory—not running down somebody that holds a world record and that's on their game. That was incredible.

Part of the reason for Lezak's comeback was the mentality of atoning for his previous two Olympic experiences in the 400 freestyle relay. He looked at his relay leg in parts, rather than as an overwhelming chore. He needed to chisel away, which is exactly how his leg unfolded. Basically, Lezak was perfect and used all 100 of his meters to come out on top.

"I started thinking, 'This guy is pretty far ahead, almost a body length. But I'm not going to give up. This is doable,'" Lezak said in analyzing the race. "I really never think at all. My best races, I've never remembered. Today, I was talking and talking to myself."

Just how remarkable was Lezak's tracking down of Bernard? Three days after the final of the 400 freestyle relay, Bernard recovered from his emotional devastation to win the gold medal in the 100 freestyle. Some argue that Bernard choked under the pressure of anchoring his country at a critical time. But a choke artist does not come back and flourish as Bernard did in the 100 free, widely considered the blue-ribbon event in the sport.

No, Lezak simply rose to the occasion like no relay swimmer before him or since. The 400 freestyle relay had been an albatross, and Lezak competed with the desire to rid himself of the burden of 2000 and 2004. Individually, he also walked away with a jubilant feeling. While Bernard won the gold medal, Lezak earned the first solo medal of his Olympic career, sharing the bronze medal in the 100 free with Brazil's Cesar Cielo.

"I was obviously shooting for the gold medal, but just to win any medal, it feels really good," Lezak said.

> It feels like everything I've done over my career has paid off. The huge mistake I made four years ago by taking the preliminaries lightly has been eating at me. For me to go out there and accomplish that medal, I'm really excited. . . . Obviously it doesn't top the relay from the other night, but it's something that has really pushed me to swim the last four years.

Lezak followed his heroics at the Beijing Games by narrowly qualifying for the 2012 Olympics in London. While he didn't get the chance to race in another championship final, Lezak competed during the preliminaries of the 400 freestyle relay. When the United States won the silver medal in the final, Lezak earned the last of his eight Olympic medals. Ironically, it was France that captured the gold medal when Yannick Agnel channeled his inner Lezak and recorded a come-from-behind victory in the closing meters.

Shortly after the London Games, Lezak announced his retirement. As he bid farewell to the sport, Lezak fondly recalled the most special moment of his career and perhaps the greatest race in swimming history.

"No matter how my individual performances went at Worlds, Olympics, and so on, I always wanted to step up on relays for the team and our country," he said. "The 400 free relay was one of the greatest moments of my career. I was a part of six consecutive years [1999–2004] of losing that relay at international competitions after the USA had never lost before, which included two Olympics. It felt great to bring the title back to the USA."

24

A Half-Stroke for History

A last-second decision to perform a half-stroke in the closing stages of his 100 butterfly duel with Serbian Milorad Cavic at the 2008 Olympics handed Michael Phelps victory by a hundredth of a second, and accounted for the seventh of his eight gold medals in Beijing.

With just a few strokes remaining in the 100-meter butterfly duel between Michael Phelps and Milorad Cavic at the 2008 Olympic Games in Beijing, Phelps's pursuit of eight gold medals looked over. Cavic had a visible lead, until Phelps dipped into his bag of magic tricks and pulled out an improbable victory.

Through six events at the 2008 Olympic Games in Beijing, Michael Phelps was perfect. With the exception of needing an epic, come-from-behind performance by anchor Jason Lezak for the United States to win the 400 freestyle relay over France, Phelps was an unstoppable force. He wasn't just winning events at the Water Cube, the nickname for the state-of-the-art Beijing Aquatic Center, he was destroying the competition, prevailing by margins typically reserved for an ahead-of-the-curve swimmer at the age-group level.

At the international level, hundredths of a second are supposed to separate the top finishers—such is the narrow difference in skill. Phelps didn't play that game. His triumphs were routs, with the rest of the field competing for silver and bronze medals. He won the 200 freestyle by nearly 2 seconds. He won the 200 and 400 individual medleys by more than a second each. Although he won the 200 butterfly by "only" 67 hundredths of a second, there was a reason: he raced the event with limited vision, his goggles having filled up with water at the start.

By the time that the final of the 100 butterfly was contested, however, Phelps was—not surprisingly—running low on energy. To that point, he had raced 15 times. Not all of his swims required maximum effort, but the totality of the events, coupled with media obligations and drug-testing procedures, had started to take their toll. Phelps and his coach, Bob Bowman, admitted to the onset of exhaustion and the importance of remaining mentally sharp to fend off the physical drain.

"I've got nothing left," Phelps said after winning the 200 individual medley. Indeed, Phelps did have some gas in the reserve tank, and he needed every ounce of that fuel for the 100 butterfly. Before the 2008 Games started, the 100 fly was viewed as the biggest individual obstacle on Phelps's road to eight gold medals. For one, it was late in the program, and a weary Phelps would clash with much fresher opponents. More, it was his only 100-meter race, and Phelps was much better suited for events that were 200 meters long or 400 meters in the case of one of the individual medley disciplines.

The biggest obstacle, however, was the presence of Serbia's Milorad Cavic, a speedster who would undoubtedly surge to a fast start in the 100 butterfly, take a sizable lead on Phelps, and try to hold on for dear life. Cavic was viewed as one of two legitimate threats to Phelps, along with American Ian Crocker, the world-record holder at the time and silver medalist to Phelps at the 2004 Olympics in Athens.

While Cavic was rising and getting faster, Crocker wasn't the force that he was in the middle of the decade, especially at the 2005 World Championships in Montreal. There, Crocker set the world record and defeated Phelps handily, with the race never in question. Like Cavic, Crocker was a fast starter, and building an advantage on Phelps during the first lap was the only way to beat him. Cavic knew all about that strategy. Brash and unafraid to speak his mind, Cavic also believed that Phelps was beatable.

"You definitely want to shoot for the gold," Cavic said 2 months before the Beijing Games.

> As much as the world would like to be entertained to see Michael Phelps get eight gold medals, I don't want to give it to him. I hope to stand in the way. I hope to slay the dragon.

I don't know if I can say that, but I did just say it. And that's kind of what it is. Everyone has this idea that he's unbeatable, and he's not. I think I'm going to have a shot.

Cavic wasn't the typical European foe of Phelps, à la Hungarian Laszlo Cseh, who was second to Phelps in Beijing in the 200 butterfly and 200 and 400 individual medleys. Unlike Cseh, born and raised in Hungary, Cavic was born in Anaheim, California, to parents who immigrated to the United States from the former Yugoslavia. He was a national–record setter for Tustin High School and was named *Swimming World Magazine*'s Male High School Swimmer of the Year in 2002. Known as Milorad on international entry and rankings lists, Cavic more frequently went by Michael or Mike while growing up and while competing collegiately for the University of California–Berkeley.

Do not be mistaken: Cavic was not ignorant to his roots. He respected his parents' heritage and the fight for freedom that gave Serbia its independence. That respect actually cost Cavic at the 2008 European Championships. After winning the 50 butterfly, Cavic protested Kosovo's recent declared independence from Serbia by wearing a T-shirt on the awards podium that read "Kosovo is Serbia." The move was deemed a political gesture by meet officials and led to Cavic's disqualification from the remainder of the meet.

Because he held dual citizenship between the United States and Serbia, Cavic had the choice of which nation to represent on the international stage. Undoubtedly, Serbia was the easier path. With the United States unmatched in its top-end talent and depth, qualifying for international competitions is viewed as difficult as competing in the international meet itself. By representing Serbia, Cavic avoided the grind faced by American swimmers.

The 100 butterfly final in Beijing took place on August 16. While Phelps was taking part in his 16th race, it was only Cavic's 4th. Earlier in the week, Cavic posted the sixth-fastest time in the preliminaries of the 100 freestyle, a Serbian record of 48.15, but withdrew before the semifinals to preserve energy for the 100 butterfly. Cavic's only other races were the prelims and semifinals of the butterfly, both of which resulted in the 6-foot-5, 200-pounder posting the fastest time of the round.

The buzz in the Water Cube before the final was at one of its highest levels of the week, the spectators well aware of what they were about to witness. They knew that Phelps was at his most vulnerable; they also knew that a Phelps victory would give him seven gold medals, tying the record achieved by Mark Spitz at the 1972 Olympics in Munich. Many Olympic experts believed that Spitz's record would never be touched, particularly with the sporting world more well rounded.

During introductions, both men showed little emotion. Cavic was in lane 4 and let out a few exhales as the television cameras followed his moves. Phelps, in lane 5, maintained his typical routine, listening to music until his name was announced. Before climbing atop their blocks, they briefly looked at each other but said nothing.

"Most guys are trembling when they have to step up to Michael Phelps," said Gary Hall Jr., the 10-time Olympic medalist who once trained with Cavic at the Race Club. "But [Cavic] did not fear him, and it showed."

As expected, Cavic bolted to the front of the field off the blocks, surfacing ahead of Phelps. The Serbian continued to pour it on over the first lap, turning in a time of 23.42, well under world-record pace. In the adjacent lane, Phelps was lagging behind. He touched the wall in 24.04 at the midway point, placing him seventh and about a half body length behind Cavic.

Using one of his patented powerful turns, Phelps cut into his deficit at the beginning of the second lap but was still trailing Cavic by a noticeable margin. Even as he picked off other swimmers between the 50- and 75-meter marks, there was a question whether he would get to Cavic. In the media section overlooking the pool, there was a tangible sense that history was coming to a close. The closer the race came to the finish, the greater the probability of a Phelps loss.

As Phelps and Cavic neared the wall for the finish, Cavic still maintained a clear edge. But on the finish, Cavic glided to the wall while Phelps took an extra half-stroke, an intuitive move that was not part of his normal routine. On most occasions, Phelps would glide to the wall, too, or get to the wall with a perfectly measured stroke. In this instance, something told him to go with a half-stroke. It proved to be a maneuver of genius.

When the final results flashed on the giant scoreboard, the Water Cube erupted. The spectators, already standing, roared their approval when it was revealed Phelps was timed in 50.58 to the 50.59 of Cavic. Somehow, Phelps had won his seventh gold medal. It was an improbable triumph and simply added another chapter to Phelps's legend. How did he pull it off?

"When I did chop the last stroke, I thought that had cost me the race," Phelps said. "But it was actually the opposite. If I had glided, I would have been way too long. I took short, faster strokes to try to get my hand on the wall. I ended up making the right decision."

Post–race Phelps comes in many forms. He has shown frustration, smirking at the scoreboard when viewing an unpleasing time. He has been nonchalant, almost void of reaction. He has smiled on occasion, allowing himself to cherish the moment. After the 100 butterfly in Beijing, Phelps was exuberant. He glanced at the scoreboard, digested its story, and shot a fist into the air. That gesture was followed by a double-handed splash of the pool. This victory was one that meant as much as any prior gold medal.

Cavic, meanwhile, had a stunned look on his face. He knew that he was out in front at the halfway point and as the swimmers neared the end of the race. He seemed confused over his second-place finish and how Phelps found a way to beat him. The Serbian delegation did not believe it either. Following the race, Serbia filed a protest and had FINA, the international governing body for swimming, view footage of the race. With the finish slowed to one frame every ten thousandth of a second, it was confirmed that Phelps won.

Sports Illustrated photographer Heinz Kluetmeier, a legend in his profession, caught the finish from above, having set up equipment that was controlled by remote. The images revealed the paper-thin tightness of the finish and have gone down in sporting lore. Cavic, though, wasn't convinced. He straddled the proverbial fence during interviews.

"I'm stoked with what happened," Cavic said. "I don't want to fight this. People will be bringing this up for years and saying you won that race. If we got to do this again, I would win it."

For all the blowout victories in his career, Phelps also had a reputation for eking out narrow decisions. At the 2004 Olympics in Athens, a storyline similar to the matchup with Cavic played out. Trailing Crocker as the swimmers neared the finish of the 100 butterfly, Phelps crept up on his American teammate and managed to get to the wall first, winning by four hundredths of a second. He also caught Crocker from behind in the 100 butterfly at the 2007 World Championships in Melbourne.

With his seventh gold medal, Phelps tied Spitz's iconic record. A day later, Phelps handled the butterfly leg on the United States' 400 medley relay and added his record-breaking eighth gold medal. Over the course of 8 days, Phelps was perfect, packaging a meet filled with overwhelming victories and drama.

There isn't a more decorated Olympian in history than Michael Phelps, who totaled 22 medals during his career, including 18 of the golden variety.

"It goes to show you that not only is this guy the greatest swimmer of all time and the greatest Olympian of all time, he's maybe the greatest athlete of all time," Spitz said. "He's the greatest racer who ever walked the planet."

Cavic got another chance at Phelps a year later, when the 2009 World Championships were held in Rome. At the time, the sport was mired in controversy over the introduction of high-tech suits, which made technology and what a swimmer was wearing more important than sheer talent. The suit dilemma, in part, stoked the rivalry between Phelps and Cavic.

First, Cavic suggested that the introduction of high-tech suits should be accepted by all and, in doing so, said that swimmers—Phelps in particular—should accept the change. He drew a parallel between the suits and the Omega timing system used at the Beijing Olympics, citing each as unfair in its own way.

"I've given this a lot of thought," Cavic said.

Throughout this whole year, I've just been hearing a lot of white noise over this suit battle. FINA has spoken. They have approved the suits. I don't like it, but they made a decision. Who knows what would have happened last year if . . . I guess what I am trying to say is technology is the problem here and I think everybody is blaming the technology.

Last year it was me and a lot of people blaming Omega for not having a better technology [in their touch pads] because I did touch the wall first, but I did not activate the wall [timing system] first. This is a problem with technology.

In addition to those comments, Cavic threw a jab at Phelps when he offered to get him a suit made by the manufacturer Arena. That suit, not Phelps's Speedo brand, was considered the best available. But Phelps remained loyal to the company that had sponsored him since his teenage years and used Cavic's words as motivation.

In the final of the 100 butterfly at the World Champs, Phelps again beat Cavic to the wall, this time setting a world record. To celebrate the win, Phelps glared at Cavic and tugged on his suit, a clear retaliation at his competitor and the words that he uttered.

"You can tell by my celebration that satisfied me a little bit," Phelps said. "I set it up perfectly. That was exactly what I wanted to do. There are always things that fire me up and motivate me. Sometimes it's a comment. Sometimes it's what people do. That's just how I tick."

After the final in Rome, Cavic finally conceded to Phelps. "I told him, 'You're the man,'" Cavic said. "He just looked at me and smiled. He knows it."

25

Age Is Just a Number

Because she defied age and excelled into her 40s, Dara Torres was dogged by doping allegations and questions during her successful comeback bids.

Despite missing out on the gold medal by a hundredth of a second in the 50-meter freestyle at the 2008 Games in Beijing, Dara Torres defied age—and became an icon for middle-aged women—by winning three silver medals at the tender age of 41.

The scene was the McDonald's Olympic Swim Stadium, site of the 1984 Games in Los Angeles. About 17,000 spectators were jammed into the stands, cheering and hollering their support for the United States, when curiosity—and the urge to support a friend—got the best of Dara Torres, then a 17-year-old preparing for the biggest race of her still-blossoming career.

Sitting in the athletes' tent, which separated the competitors from the competition venue, Torres pulled back a corner of the tent to catch a glimpse of Rowdy Gaines's race and the atmosphere that soon encompassed her as a member of the United States' 400 freestyle relay. What Torres saw was an overwhelming sight. "I remember lifting up the bottom and seeing 17,000 people and I just freaked out," Torres said during an interview years later. "I got hot. I had to go to the nurse's station. They were putting ice packs on me."

Torres was so rattled by what she witnessed, her performance in the morning preliminaries was a nightmare. Although the United States easily advanced to the final, the coaching staff contemplated replacing Torres for the evening session, only to decide otherwise. To her credit and with the support of older teammates, Torres gathered herself and performed admirably in the final, producing a lifetime-best split as the United States surged to the gold medal.

Twenty-four years after making her Olympic debut, as Torres competed at the 2008 Olympic Games in Beijing (her fifth Olympiad), it was hard to believe that she was ever a nervous wreck in international competition. In Beijing, there was nary a hint of nerves. Rather, the woman who walked the deck of the Water Cube—and was old enough to be the mother of many of her rivals and teammates—was the definition of confidence and focus.

When the 2008 Olympics are discussed, Michael Phelps's name immediately highlights the conversation. That is not a startling development considering that Phelps won eight gold medals in Beijing, eclipsing the seven gold medals captured by Mark Spitz at the 1972 Games in Munich. Making Phelps's achievement even more impressive was the fact that two of his triumphs—the 400 freestyle relay and 100 butterfly—were earned with dramatic finishes.

As dominant as Phelps was, the woman whom he jokingly referred to as "mom" occupied her share of headlines. It was difficult to fathom the fact that, as a 41-year-old, Torres was competing in a fifth Olympiad, let alone landing on the podium. By this point in a career, most women are a decade removed from the sport, if not longer. Torres, though, is far from an ordinary woman.

More than three decades ago, Torres's name first started to make the rounds in swimming circles as she established age-group records in the sprint events. Anyone familiar with her raw talent, found in a 5-foot-11 frame, knew that she had Olympic ability, talent that revealed itself as she qualified for relay duty at the 1984 Games.

From 1984 through 1992, Torres was a regular on the American Olympic roster. Her gold medal in the 400 free relay from 1984 was complemented by a silver medal in the 400 medley relay and bronze in the 400 freestyle relay in 1988 and a gold in the 400 freestyle relay in 1992. Then, Torres was gone, off to pursue other endeavors, including modeling opportunities and television reporting gigs.

Like many swimmers of that time, Torres was not going to hang around in a sport known for early retirement. With Torres's good looks opening other doors, she was making a fiscally smart decision to move on. With four Olympic medals to her name, she constructed a solid career, albeit one that was not going to stand out when lined up against the great American females.

For 7 years following the 1992 Olympics, Torres was comfortable with her life and uninterested in a return to the pool. Then the itch took effect, prompting Torres to make the first of what was a pair of comebacks. Joining forces with legendary coach Richard Quick, the head man at Stanford University and its offshoot club program, Torres began pursuit of a berth to the 2000 Olympic Games in Sydney.

"When I first decided to come back, I told my coach, 'Let's be realistic. I just want to make a relay.' I just want to go there and make the team and just want to have fun and swim my heart out, swim as fast as I can," Torres said.

If Torres truly meant what she said, she thoroughly exceeded her expectations. As the 2000 Olympic Trials neared, Torres continually displayed potential for a major haul in Sydney. She broke the American record in the 50 freestyle at the Santa Clara International Meet, a tune-up for Trials, and went on to qualify for the Sydney Games in the 50 and 100 freestyles, 100 butterfly, and two relays. At the age of 33, which was considered dinosaur-esque, Torres was redefining what was possible for a female swimmer deemed to be past her prime.

Even Quick, who coached some of the greatest athletes in the sport's history, had a difficult time digesting Torres's excellence. Simply, it was a combination of sheer skill and desire. So hungry was Torres to excel in her first comeback that she had to be separated from teammate Jenny Thompson—an Olympic great—in training sessions, so intense were the practice duels.

"I've never seen anything like that in my life, in any sport, to be out of the sport for seven years and to come back like that," Quick said of Torres's second career. "Not that I wasn't confident, but if you had asked me a year ago if she would be breaking records and swimming like that, I wouldn't have believed you."

Against the best that the sport had to offer in Sydney, Torres bettered her career medal haul heading into the meet by claiming five medals. In addition to helping the United States to gold medals in the 400 freestyle relay and 400 medley relay, Torres added individual bronze medals in the 50 and 100 freestyles and 100 butterfly.

She was as good as she had ever been. Yet, Sydney was the end as far as she was concerned. Retirement called again, with many bidding farewell in astonishment over the vast exploits of a 33-year-old. What they didn't realize was they hadn't seen anything yet.

Once again, Torres was a spectator, content to watch the American team compete at the Athens Games in 2004. Torres had more important focuses in her life, including the birth of her daughter, Tessa, in 2006. But it was the birth of her daughter that led to a second comeback. Initially seeking exercise opportunities, the water called Torres back to compete. Initially, there were question marks to the seriousness of her quest, but when Torres started uncorking world-class times, the doubts dissipated.

There were a handful of meets that changed Torres's initial pursuit of a relay bid to the Beijing Games. First, she shined in a pair of competitions in Europe, posting a sizzling time in the 100 freestyle in Rome, then winning the 50 freestyle during the Monte Carlo stop on the Mare Nostrum Series.

Add in an American record in the 50 freestyle at the 2007 U.S. Summer Nationals and a triumph in the 100 freestyle over an impressive field, and the expectations for Torres had been altered. It was Beijing or bust.

"When I went the [54.61] in Rome, everything changed," Torres said. "I never expected that. I was so nervous before the final. It was like I was starting all over. I touched the wall and heard the crowd, but when I looked up at the scoreboard, my eyes bugged out. I was in complete shock . . . I started thinking about individual events [in Beijing]."

At the 2008 Olympics in Beijing, 41-year-old Dara Torres won a silver medal in the 50 freestyle, falling short of gold by a hundredth of a second.

The route to the Beijing Games was hardly an easy one for Torres. Although the financially well-off Torres employed a unique team of trainers and physical therapists, she was still a 40-something woman whose muscles and body did not bounce back as quickly as when she was a youngster and was capable of handling an intense workload. Somehow, though, she fended off decline in a way that others haven't been able to.

Torres was also constantly subjected to finger-pointing, accusations from near and far claiming that she could not possibly compete at an elite level without the aid of performance-enhancing drugs. Since she knew that the doping accusations were unavoidable, Torres simply rolled with the punches. When a new claim was levied against her, she did nothing more than reaffirm that she was drug-free, and she pointed to the fact that she made herself available to enhanced testing and more frequent testing than most other athletes.

"I'm an open book," Torres said in the lead-up to the 2008 Games. "DNA test me, blood test me, urine test me. Do whatever you want. I want to show people I'm clean. So if anyone says it now—I mean, I'm being blood tested and urine tested—I just take it as a compliment."

After much hoopla, the summer of 2008 finally allowed Torres to show the incredible nature of the human body. She was sensational at the Olympic Trials in Omaha, Nebraska, winning both the 50 and 100 freestyles, the latter event also handing Torres berths on the American 400 freestyle and 400 medley relays in Beijing. Concerned that her body could not withstand three additional races in the 100 freestyle at the Olympics, Torres withdrew from that event, leaving her with three events at the 2008 Games. Those events had a silver lining.

Torres started her Beijing program by handling the anchor leg on the American 400 freestyle relay, which finished second to the Netherlands. After that opener, Torres served as a Team USA cheerleader for nearly a week, until she got back in the water for the 50 freestyle. Cruising through the preliminaries and semifinals of the one-lap dash, Torres entered the final as a legitimate contender for the gold medal. The smallest margin of time in the sport left her just short.

In what is the most frenetic event in the sport, Torres and Germany's Britta Steffen battled stroke for stroke with the gold medal on the line—with Steffen getting to the wall in 24.06 and Torres grabbing the silver medal in an American-record effort of 24.07. If not for a poor finish, in which Torres hit the touchpad with her palm rather than extended fingers, she might have had an individual Olympic crown. Regardless, she became the oldest medalist in swimming history.

"It feels pretty good," Torres said. "I'm competitive, so I wanted to win gold in the 50. I gave it my best shot. Maybe I shouldn't have filed my nails last night."

About 35 minutes after the 50 freestyle, Torres was on the deck again, this time anchoring the United States to the silver medal in the 400 medley relay. Although she could not catch Australian anchor Libby Trickett, Torres turned in the fastest 100 freestyle relay split in history, further testament to her age-defying ways. The medley relay gave Torres the 12th medal of her Olympic career, which tied Jenny Thompson for the most by a woman in swimming history.

"Dara Torres never ceases to amaze me," said Mark Schubert, the general manager of USA Swimming and a coach to Torres during her teenage years. "The only reason she could do this is she's never been out of shape a day in her life. She loves to train and be fit."

Four years after her Beijing exploits, Torres returned to the U.S. Trials for a run at a sixth Olympiad, only to fall short as a 45-year-old with a fourth-place finish in the 50 freestyle. As much as it pained her to miss out on a trip to London, Torres recognized the importance of her presence.

For Torres, her career was equal parts athlete and inspiration.

"If it helps anyone else out there who is in their middle-aged years, and they put off something they thought they couldn't do because they were too old or maybe thought that because they have children they can't balance what they want to do and be a parent, then I'm absolutely thrilled," she said.

GRAPH 25.1

When Dara Torres won the silver medal in the 50 freestyle at the 2008 Olympic Games in Beijing, she did more than add to her legacy, which is defined by 12 Olympic medals. The 41-year-old Torres also proved that age—while sometimes difficult to overcome—does not have to mean a decline in skill. Here's a look at the ages of the eight women in the final of the 50 freestyle.

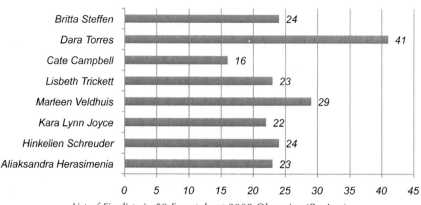

List of Finalists in 50 Freestyle at 2008 Olympics (By Age)

Under Consideration

The Moments That Just Missed

Given the 100-year-plus history of the Olympic Games, there were several moments that received consideration for inclusion in this work. Although these moments did not make the final cut, they deserve a brief mention. Here is a look at some of the other great Olympic moments, listed in chronological order.

THE FIRST OLYMPIC CHAMPION (1896)

The modern Olympics launched in 1896 in Athens, and no one will ever take the following distinction from Hungarian Alfred Hajos: first Olympic champion. Racing against waves and cold temperatures in the Mediterranean Sea, Hajos—already a European champion—won gold medals in the 100 and 1200 freestyles. The Hungarian had designs on winning the 500 freestyle as well, but that event was scheduled between the 100 and 1200 distances, making pursuit of a triple an impossible task.

BREAK OUT THE BROOM (1920)

Only three women's events were contested at the 1920 Olympics in Antwerp, Belgium, and the record books show that American Ethelda Bleibtrey was victorious in each of them. In what is surely to be the last sweep of the events by any athlete given today's expansive schedule, Bleibtrey collected individual gold medals in the 100 and 300 freestyles and helped the United States to the gold medal in the 400 freestyle relay. Making her meet even more impressive was the fact that each of her triumphs arrived in world-record time.

BEFORE REPEATING WAS IN STYLE (1928)

One record will never be able to be taken from the United States' Martha Norelius, a star during the first half of the 20th century. While Duke Kahanamoku and Johnny Weissmuller were repeat Olympic champions, Norelius was the first woman to pull off the feat, winning the 400 freestyle at the 1924 and 1928 Games. Her second win in the event was a rout, as Norelius beat the Netherlands' Marie Braun by 15 seconds.

WILL THE TRUE WINNER PLEASE STAND UP? (1960)

With electronic timing still developing at the time of the 1960 Olympics in Rome, lane judges were used as the primary timers and decision makers. For Australian John Devitt and American Lance Larson, human error played a huge role in the biggest race of their lives.

When Devitt and Larson neared the finish of the 100 freestyle, it was nearly impossible to determine which man got his hand on the wall first. Two of the three judges charged with determining the first-place finisher had Devitt narrowly in front. However, two of the three judges given the task of determining the second-place finisher had Devitt in that position, meaning that they believed that Larson was the winner. Meanwhile, the three timers all had Larson in first place, with the electronic timing system agreeing with Larson as the victor.

When chief judge Hans Runstromer got involved, he declared Devitt as the gold medalist and Larson as the silver medalist. The United States quickly appealed Runstromer's decision but to no avail, leaving the outcome of the 100 freestyle at the 1960 Games as one of the most controversial finishes in the history of the sport.

A PAINFUL GOLD MEDAL (1964)

The cliché "No pain, no gain" is often heard in sports, but it probably fits American Dick Roth better than anyone else. At the 1964 Olympics in Tokyo, Roth was stricken with a nasty case of appendicitis, causing him searing pain. But with the 400 individual medley on Roth's radar, he refused to undergo necessary surgery until after his event.

Fighting through the pain of his illness and the pain caused by the decathlon of swimming, Roth managed to not only finish his race but earn the gold medal in a world-record time. It was a truly heroic effort by Roth, who beat his American teammate Roy Saari by nearly 2 seconds.

MONSTER OF THE WAVES (1988)

Politics and sports go together about as well as Chicken McNuggets and a vintage wine, the leading example of the mismatch being the United States' decision to boycott the 1980 Olympics in opposition of the Soviet Union's invasion of Afghanistan. That decision by President Jimmy Carter robbed numerous athletes of the opportunity to excel on the biggest stage, including the likes of future Olympic champions Tracy Caulkins, Mary T. Meagher, and Rowdy Gaines.

Although the move by President Carter is the best known of the ill-advised political decisions related to sports, it is worth noting that 4 years later, Eastern Bloc nations united and boycotted the 1984 Games in Los Angeles as a retaliatory maneuver. With the Soviet Union at the forefront of this boycott, distance great Vladimir Salnikov was denied the chance to defend his Olympic crowns in the 400 and 1500 freestyles. Whether he would get another Olympic chance seemed tenuous at best.

However, when the 1988 Games unfolded in Seoul, Salnikov summoned his immense talent and captured a second gold medal in the 1500 freestyle, a feat deemed superhuman since 8 years had passed since his initial Olympic triumph. Salnikov's victory was so revered that he received a standing ovation from his fellow Olympians when he ventured into the athletes' dining hall hours after his second coronation.

Whether Salnikov would have won the gold medal in 1984 rather than American Mike O'Brien is nothing more than conjecture. What is not disputable is the special moment that Salnikov delivered in Seoul, proving that a politically generated hiatus could not stop a legend.

A CELEBRATION AT HOME (1992)

Although born in the United States and trained at the prestigious Bolles School in Florida, Martin Zubero never lost touch with his Spanish roots. In fact, Zubero held dual citizenship and ultimately opted to represent Spain—the birthplace of his father—in international competition. So when the 1992 Games were designated for Barcelona, a special opportunity was afforded to Zubero, a chance that he fulfilled in fine form.

At the Barcelona Games, Zubero became the first Spanish swimmer—and still the only—to capture a gold medal. Competing in the 200 backstroke, Zubero covered the distance in 1:58.47 and sent the spectators in Barcelona into a party atmosphere as they celebrated a victory by one of their own.

"It meant a lot to me since my father's side of the family is Spanish," Zubero said. "There was a ton of pressure on me to win the 200 backstroke since I was the world champion and world-record holder going into the Games. To win the gold in Spain was a dream and I was very fortunate to have the support of the Spanish people to cheer me on to the gold."

MIGHTY MOUSE (1996)

When Hungary's Krisztina Egerszegi won the 1996 Olympic gold medal in the 200 backstroke in Atlanta, she accomplished a feat that had been achieved only one previous time in the sport's history: she captured three consecutive gold medals in the same event. Only Australian Dawn Fraser (1956–1964) in the 100 freestyle had ruled an event over three straight Olympiads.

Egerszegi did not just prevail in Olympic competition; she buried the opposition. She won her first title by more than a second and bested the competition by more than 2 seconds at the 1992 Games. In her history-making triumph, Egerszegi was victorious by more than 4 seconds, a fitting way to cap what was a dominant career.

SOUTH AFRICAN SURGE (2004)

Just 12 years after making its return to the Olympic stage following years of an International Olympic Committee ban due to its apartheid policies, South Africa registered one of the biggest athletic achievements in its nation's history at the 2004 Games in Athens. Four years after Australia broke the United States' stranglehold on the 400 freestyle relay, South Africa lengthened the Americans' absence from the top of the podium.

Fueled by a sensational opening leg by Roland Schoeman, the squad of Schoeman, Lyndon Ferns, Darian Townsend, and Ryk Neethling set a world record of 3:13.17 and prevailed by more than a second over the Netherlands, with the United States taking the bronze medal.

"This was our day," Schoeman said. "As the movie says, 'any given Sunday.' For the relay, I told the guys, this is our Sunday."

MISSY THE MISSILE (2012)

The best of Missy Franklin is almost certainly still to come, but at the 2012 Olympics, the American teenager provided a glimpse of her incredible talent. Picking up five medals, including four gold, Franklin was one of the stars of the London Games. She won titles in the 100 and 200 backstrokes and helped the United States to gold in a pair of relays and to bronze in another.

Nothing showed Franklin's youthfulness more than the way that she handled a difficult double on the third night of competition. After advancing to the final of the 200 freestyle, Franklin had only 13 minutes of recovery time before contesting the final of the 100 backstroke. Despite that tight window, and using the diving well adjacent to the competition pool for warm-down purposes, Franklin had enough energy in her tank to overhaul Australian Emily Seebohm in the latter stages of the race and win gold in the 100 backstroke.

"I dreamed about this moment my whole life," Franklin said of her gold in the 100 backstroke. "I finally got one after 17 years!"

Appendix A

The Olympic Games—Years, Sites, and Dates

Year	Site	Dates
1896	Athens, Greece	Apr 6–15
1900	Paris, France	May 20–Oct 28
1904	St. Louis, Missouri	Jul 1–Nov 23
1906	Athens, Greece	Apr 22–May 2
1908	London, England	Apr 27–Oct 31
1912	Stockholm, Sweden	May 5–Jul 27
1920	Antwerp, Belgium	Apr 23–Sept 12
1924	Paris, France	May 4–Jul 27
1928	Amsterdam, Netherlands	May 17–Aug 12
1932	Los Angeles, California	Jul 30–Aug 14
1936	Berlin, Germany	Aug 1–16
1948	London, England	Jul 29–Aug 14
1952	Helsinki, Finland	Jul 19–Aug 3
1956	Melbourne, Australia	Nov 22–Dec 8
1960	Rome, Italy	Aug 25–Sep 11
1964	Tokyo, Japan	Oct 10–24
1968	Mexico City, Mexico	Oct 12–27
1972	Munich, Germany	Aug 26–Sep 11
1976	Montreal, Canada	Jul 17–Aug 1
1980	Moscow, Russia	Jul 19–Aug 3
1984	Los Angeles, California	Jul 28–Aug 12
1988	Seoul, South Korea	Sep 17–Oct 5
1992	Barcelona, Spain	Jul 25–Aug 9
1996	Atlanta, Georgia	Jul 20–Aug 4
2000	Sydney, Australia	Sep 14–Oct 1
2004	Athens, Greece	Aug 13–29
2008	Beijing, China	Aug 8–24
2012	London, England	Jul 27–Aug 12

Appendix B

Most Overall Medals—By Country

Country	No.	Gold	Silver	Bronze
United States	520	230	164	126
Australia	178	57	60	61
East Germany	92	38	32	22
Japan	73	20	24	29
Great Britain	67	15	22	30
Hungary	66	25	23	18
Germany	59	13	18	28
Soviet Union	59	12	21	26
Netherlands	56	19	18	19
Canada	42	7	14	21
France	40	8	13	19
China	37	12	17	8
Sweden	35	8	14	13
West Germany	22	3	5	14
Russia	19	5	7	7
Italy	17	4	4	9
South Africa	15	6	3	6
Brazil	13	1	4	8
Denmark	12	2	5	5
Unified Germany	12	1	5	6
Austria	11	1	6	4
Unified Team	10	6	3	1
Ukraine	10	4	5	1

Appendix C

Most Gold Medals—Career

Name	No.
Michael Phelps, U.S.	18
Mark Spitz, U.S.	9
Jenny Thompson, U.S.	8
Matt Biondi, U.S.	8
Kristin Otto, East Germany	6
Amy Van Dyken, U.S.	6
Ryan Lochte, U.S.	5
Gary Hall Jr., U.S.	5
Ian Thorpe, Australia	5
Aaron Peirsol, U.S.	5
Krisztina Egerszegi, Hungary	5
Tom Jager, U.S.	5
Don Schollander, U.S.	5
Johnny Weissmuller, U.S.	5

Appendix D

Most Medals—Career

Name	No.	Gold	Silver	Bronze
Michael Phelps, U.S.	22	18	2	2
Jenny Thompson, U.S.	12	8	3	1
Dara Torres, U.S.	12	4	4	4
Natalie Coughlin, U.S.	12	3	4	5
Mark Spitz, U.S.	11	9	1	1
Matt Biondi, U.S.	11	8	2	1
Ryan Lochte, U.S.	11	5	3	3
Gary Hall Jr., U.S.	10	5	3	2
Franziska van Almsick, Germany	10	0	4	6
Ian Thorpe, Australia	9	5	3	1
Alexander Popov, Russia	9	4	5	0
Leisel Jones, Australia	9	3	5	1
Dawn Fraser, Australia	8	4	4	0
Kornelia Ender, East Germany	8	4	4	0
Roland Matthes, East Germany	8	4	2	2
Inge De Bruijn, Holland	8	4	2	2
Jason Lezak, U.S.	8	4	2	2
Petria Thomas, Australia	8	3	4	1
Shirley Babashoff, U.S.	8	2	6	0
Susie O'Neill, Australia	8	2	4	2
Aaron Peirsol, U.S.	7	5	2	0
Krisztina Egerszegi, Hungary	7	5	1	1
Tom Jager, U.S.	7	5	1	1
Charles Daniels, U.S.	7	4	1	2
Kosuke Kitajima, Japan	7	4	1	2
Libby Trickett, Australia	7	4	1	2
Pieter van den Hoogenband, Holland	7	3	2	2
Amanda Beard, U.S.	7	2	4	1
Kirsty Coventry, Zimbabwe	7	2	4	1

Appendix E

Most Gold Medals—Single Olympiad

Name	No.	Year
Michael Phelps, U.S.	8	2008
Mark Spitz, U.S.	7	1972
Michael Phelps, U.S.	6	2004
Kristin Otto, East Germany	6	1988
Matt Biondi, U.S.	5	1988
Michael Phelps, U.S.	4	2012
Missy Franklin, U.S.	4	2012
Amy Van Dyken, U.S.	4	1996
John Naber, U.S.	4	1976
Don Schollander, U.S.	4	1964

Appendix F

Most Medals—Single Olympiad

Year	Name	No.	Gold	Silver	Bronze
2008	Michael Phelps, U.S.	8	8	0	0
2004	Michael Phelps, U.S.	8	6	0	2
1972	Mark Spitz, U.S.	7	7	0	0
1988	Matt Biondi, U.S.	7	5	1	1
1988	Kristin Otto, East Germany	6	6	0	0
2012	Michael Phelps, U.S.	6	4	2	0
2008	Natalie Coughlin, U.S.	6	1	2	3
1976	Kornelia Ender, East Germany	5	4	1	0
2012	Missy Franklin, U.S.	5	4	0	1
2000	Ian Thorpe, Australia	5	3	1	1
1904	Charles Daniels, U.S.	5	3	1	1
1972	Shane Gould, Australia	5	3	1	1
2012	Allison Schmitt, U.S.	5	3	1	1
2012	Ryan Lochte, U.S.	5	2	2	1
2004	Natalie Coughlin, U.S.	5	2	2	1
1980	Ines Diers, East Germany	5	2	2	1
2000	Dara Torres, U.S.	5	2	0	3
1976	Shirley Babashoff, U.S.	5	1	4	0
2012	Alicia Coutts, Australia	5	1	3	1

Bibliography

BOOKS AND ARTICLES

"Anthony Nesty: Gators and Gold Medals." Florida Swim Network. October 21, 2013. http:// floridaswimnetwork.com/2013/10/21/anthony-nesty-gators-and-gold-medals/

Bayles, Fred. "Seoul Spotlight." Associated Press. September 19, 1988. http://www.apnews archive.com/1988/Seoul-Spotlight/id-cfb1f13bf7268e532c5c3320afd3f7fe

Biondi, Matt. "Diary of a Champion." *Sports Illustrated*. October 3, 1988. http://sportsillus trated.cnn.com/vault/article/magazine/MAG1067810/index.htm

Brennan, Christine. "Keeping Score: 25 Years Later, Boycott Gnaws at Athletes." *USA Today*. April 13, 2005. http://usatoday30.usatoday.com/sports/columnist/brennan/2005-04-13-bren nan_x.htm

Caple, Jim. "How Can One Not Be Won Over by Phelps' Feat?" ESPN.com. August 17, 2008. http://sports.espn.go.com/oly/summer08/columns/story?columnist=caple_jim&id=3539430

Carter, Jimmy. "Speech on Afghanistan." Miller Center. January 4, 1980. http://millercenter .org/president/speeches/detail/3403

Clarey, Christopher. "Cavic Finds a Personal Triumph in the Narrowest of Defeats." *New York Times*. August 16, 2008. http://www.nytimes.com/2008/08/17/sports/olympics/17cavic.html

Commings, Jeff. "Anthony Nesty among Talented Coaching Staff at Florida." *Swimming World Magazine*. May 30, 2013. http://www.swimmingworldmagazine.com/lane9/news /morningswimshow/34548.asp

Cowley, Michael. "I Touched the Wall Before Phelps, Says Cavic." *Sydney Morning Herald*. July 28, 2009. http://www.smh.com.au/news/sport/swimming/i-touched-the-wall-before -phelps-says-cavic/2009/07/28/1248546705663.html

———. "Klim Relives the Night We Smashed Them like Guitars." *Sydney Morning Herald*. September 8, 2010. http://www.smh.com.au/sport/swimming/klim-relives-the-night-we -smashed-them-like-guitars-20100907-14zms.html

Davies, Lisa. "I Killed My Mother, Dawn Fraser Tells Interviewer." Australian National News Wire. August 9, 2004. http://web.ebscohost.com/ehost/detail?vid=8&sid=9686336e-7641 -4699-abd3-b542ab290e31%40sessionmgr115&hid=4212&bdata=JnNpdGU9ZWhvc3 QtbGl2ZQ%3d%3d#db=n5h&AN=74C3111855517

De George, Matthew. *Duels in the Pool: Swimming's Greatest Rivalries.* Lanham, MD: Scarecrow Press, 2013.

Dillman, Lisa. "Gold Feat." *Los Angeles Times.* September 17, 2000. http://articles.latimes.com/2000/sep/17/news/ss-22673

———. "A Team Player Who Rises to the Challenge." *Los Angeles Times.* August 12, 2008. http://articles.latimes.com/2008/aug/12/sports/sp-olylezak12

Dodd, Mike. "Lezak Ties For Bronze; Bernard Wins 100-Meter Men's Freestyle." *USA Today.* August 14, 2008. http://usatoday30.usatoday.com/sports/olympics/beijing/swimming/2008-08-13-100-meter-freestyle_n.htm

Dodds, Tracy. "Morales Is Third, Loses His Place." *Los Angeles Times.* August 10, 1988. http://articles.latimes.com/1988-08-10/sports/sp-283_1_pablo-morales

———. "The Paper Chase Can Wait: Pablo Morales Puts Off Law School to Devote a Year to the Olympics." *Los Angeles Times.* August 7, 1988. http://articles.latimes.com/1988-08-07/sports/sp-406_1_pablo-morales

Dwyre, Bill. "Montgomery Hits 49.99." *Milwaukee Journal.* July 26, 1976. http://news.google.com/newspapers?nid=1499&dat=19760726&id=RPwjAAAAIBAJ&sjid=jH4EAAAAIBAJ&pg=5607,2895938

Eldridge, Larry. "Hanging On Was Worth Effort for Olympic Swimmer Rowdy Gaines." *Christian Science Monitor.* January 25, 1985. http://www.csmonitor.com/1985/0125/prowdy.html

"Eric Moussambani Flails Way to Glory." *The Guardian.* July 2012. http://www.guardian.co.uk/sport/blog/2012/jan/25/olympic-games-eric-eel-moussambani

"FINA Changes Rules after Athens Controversy." *ABC News.* July 23, 2005. http://www.abc.net.au/news/2005-07-23/fina-changes-rules-after-athens-controversy/2064972

Fitzpatrick, Frank. "Sharing the Gold." *Philadelphia Inquirer.* September 23, 2000. http://articles.philly.com/2000-09-23/sports/25583746_1_anthony-ervin-hoogenband-dead-heat

———. "U.S. Shut Out in 100 Freestyle." *Philadelphia Inquirer.* August 18, 2004. http://articles.philly.com/2004-08-18/sports/25391533_1_hoogenband-lezak-and-ian-crocker-australian-ian-thorpe

"Forbes Carlile." *Talking Heads with Peter Thompson.* August 4, 2008. http://www.abc.net.au/tv/talkingheads/txt/s2316987.htm

Fraser, Dawn. *What I Learned along the Way.* Sydney, Australia: New Holland, 2013.

Frenette, Gene. "Hogshead Rose to the Surface." Jacksonville.com. n.d. http://jacksonville.com/special/athletes_of_century/stories/hogshead.shtml

Fyodorov, Gennady. "Soviet Bloc Tit-for-Tat Sank L.A." *Moscow Times.* July 18, 1996. http://www.themoscowtimes.com/news/article/soviet-bloc-tit-for-tat-sank-la/321279.html

Gelman, Mitch. "Hall Jr., Ervin Share Gold in 50; Dutchman Takes Bronze." CNNSI.com. September 22, 2000. http://sportsillustrated.cnn.com/olympics/2000/swimming/news/2000/09/22/mens_50m/

Gordos, Phil. "Thorpe Steals Phelps' Thunder." *BBC Sport.* August 17, 2004. http://news.bbc.co.uk/sport2/hi/olympics_2004/swimming/3571978.stm

Grasswill, Helen. "When Harry Met Dawn." *Australian Story.* June 5, 2002. http://www.abc.net.au/austory/transcripts/s544221.htm

Gustafson, Mike. "Acknowledging Enith Brigitha." USA Swimming. February 15, 2012. http://www.usaswimming.org/ViewNewsArticle.aspx?TabId=1&itemid=4181&mid=8712

Hall, Gary. "We Have Our Work Cut Out for Us." CNNSI.com. August 22, 2000. http://sportsillustrated.cnn.com/olympics/news/2000/08/22/hall_five/

Hitchings, Anna. "Olympic Swimmer Dawn Fraser Releases New Autobiography." *Daily Telegraph*. November 19, 2013. http://www.dailytelegraph.com.au/newslocal/inner-west/olympic -swimmer-dawn-fraser-releases-new-autobiography/story-fngr8h4f-1226763192440

Jerardi, Dick. "Morales: I Never Imagined This out of Retirement; He's Back in the Swim." *Philadelphia Daily News*. July 24, 1992. http://articles.philly.com/1992-07-24 /sports/26028788_1_swimmers-in-american-history-bud-greenspan-pablo-morales

King, Helen. "Fanny Durack." *Australian Dictionary of Biography*. 1981. http://adb.anu.edu .au/biography/durack-sarah-fanny-6063

Kirshenbaum, Jerry. "Fastest Splash in the West." *Sports Illustrated*, July 19, 1971, 18–19.

———. "A Feat of Olympian Proportions." *Sports Illustrated*, August 23, 1976, 14–15.

———. "The Golden Days of Mark the Shark." *Sports Illustrated*, September 11, 1972, 27–31.

———. "She's on Top Down Under." *Sports Illustrated*, March 13, 1972, 28–36.

Levin, Dan. "She's Set Her Sights on L.A." *Sports Illustrated*, June 18, 1984, 40–48.

Litsky, Frank. "Biondi Is Learning to Set His Pace." *New York Times*. March 25, 1988. http:// www.nytimes.com/1988/03/25/sports/biondi-is-learning-to-set-his-pace.html

Lohn, John. "Biondi Reflects on Golden High-Water Mark." SwimVortex. May 15, 2013. http://www.swimvortex.com/biondi-reflects-on-golden-high-water-mark/

———. "Just Call Him Rowdy." *Swimming World Magazine*. August 5, 2009. http://www .swimmingworldmagazine.com/lane9/news/21988.asp

———. "Strong Arm of Armstrong and Lawrence." SwimVortex. May 21, 2013. http://www .swimvortex.com/when-armstrong-lawrence-ruled-the-pool/

———. *They Ruled the Pool: The 100 Greatest Swimmers in History*. Lanham, MD: Scarecrow Press, 2013.

Longman, Jere. "Australia Aglow as Young Star Gets Two Golds." *New York Times*. September 17, 2000. http://www.nytimes.com/2000/09/17/sports/sydney-2000-swimming-australia -aglow-as-young-star-gets-two-golds.html

Lord, Craig. "Courage on the Blocks." *Times of London*. September 19, 2000.

———. "What a Week That Was for Pioneer Fanny Durack." SwimVortex. July 10, 2013. http://www.swimvortex.com/what-a-week-that-was-for-pioneer-fanny-durack/

Manning, Anita. "Hall Won't Let Diabetes Sink Successful Swimming Career." *USA Today*. July 29, 2004. http://usatoday30.usatoday.com/sports/olympics/athens/swimming/2004 -07-29-hall-jr-diabetes_x.htm

McMullen, Paul. *Amazing Pace: The Story of Olympic Champion Michael Phelps from Sydney to Athens to Beijing*. New York: Rodale, 2006.

———. "It's a Two-Man Race, and Then Some." *Baltimore Sun*. August 16, 2004. http://articles .baltimoresun.com/2004-08-16/sports/0408160130_1_den-hoogenband-thorpe-phelps

Miles, Janelle. "Dawn's Golden Record Forty Years On: Dawn Fraser's Feat of Winning Gold in the Same Event at Three Olympics Still Inspires Awe." *Townsville Bulletin*. June 26, 2004. http://web.ebscohost.com/ehost/detail?vid=8&sid=9686336e-7641-4699-abd3-b54 2ab290e31%40sessionmgr115&hid=123&bdata=JnNpdGU9ZWhvc3QtbGl2ZQ%3d% 3d#db=n5h&AN=200406261030361229

Montague, James. "'Eric the Eel' Dreams of Olympic Return.'" *CNN*. July 31, 2012. http:// edition.cnn.com/2012/07/31/sport/olympics-2012-eric-eel-moussambani

Montville, Leigh. "Bravo, Pablo." *Sports Illustrated*. August 3, 1992. http://si.com/vault /article/magazine/MAG1004059/index.htm

Morgan, Piers. "Interview with Mark Spitz." *Piers Morgan Tonight*. July 14, 2012. http:// transcripts.cnn.com/TRANSCRIPTS/1207/14/pmt.01.html

Muckenfuss, Mark. "Olympic Swimming, 1984." *Swimming World Magazine*. September 1984. http://www.swimmingworldmagazine.com/interactive/Rowdy_Gaines.pdf

Newberry, Paul. "Ervin, Swimming's Mystery Man, Returns to the Pool." Associated Press. May 18, 2012. http://bigstory.ap.org/content/ervin-swimmings-mystery-man-returns-pool

O'Mahony, Jennifer. "How Eric 'The Eel' Moussambani Inspired a Generation in Swimming Pool at Sydney Games." *Telegraph*. July 27, 2012. http://www.telegraph.co.uk/sport/olympics/swimming/9432830/London-2012-Olympics-how-Eric-the-Eel-Moussambani-inspired-a-generation-in-swimming-pool-at-Sydney-Games.html

"Peirsol: Kitajima Used Illegal Kick." Associated Press. August 15, 2004. http://sports.espn.go.com/oly/summer04/swimming/news/story?id=1859947

"Phenomenal Phelps Wins Seventh Gold by .01 Seconds to Tie Spitz." Associated Press. August 16, 2008. http://sports.espn.go.com/oly/summer08/swimming/news/story?id=3537831

Powers, John. "Probe Reveals that East German Athletes Used Performance Drugs." *Cedartown Standard*, December 15, 1998, 3B.

Rattie, Jim. "Ahead of Her Time, Debbie Meyer Didn't Cash in on Olympic Success, but She's a Hall of Famer." *Sacramento Bee*, September 20, 1987, C2.

Reid, Scott. "1980 Olympic Profile: Brian Goodell." *Orange County Register*. July 16, 2010. http://www.ocregister.com/articles/goodell-258087-olympic-carter.html

Robb, Sharon. "An Olympic Veteran's Day: Morales, 27, Earns Gold." *Sun Sentinel*. July 28, 1992. http://articles.sun-sentinel.com/1992-07-28/sports/9202210948_1_first-olympic-race-olympic-and-world-olympic-record

———. "Pablo's Private Passion." *Sun Sentinel*. July 23, 1992. http://articles.sun-sentinel.com/1992-07-23/specialsection/9202210182_1_trials-pablo-morales-law-school

Robinson, Charles. "Frenchman Fires Up U.S. Relay Team." *Yahoo Sports*. August 8, 2008. http://sports.yahoo.com/olympics/beijing/swimming/news?slug=cr-french-trash-080808

———. "Lezak Lifts U.S. In 'Best-Ever' Relay." *Yahoo Sports*. August 11, 2008. http://sports.yahoo.com/olympics/beijing/swimming/news?slug=cr-swimbestever081108

Ruane, Michael E. "Phelps' Quest for Seven Golds Is Swept Away." *Washington Post*. August 17, 2004. http://www.washingtonpost.com/wp-dyn/articles/A5222-2004Aug16.html

"Shane Gould." *Enough Rope with Andrew Denton*. March 29, 2004. http://www.abc.net.au/tv/enoughrope/transcripts/s1076428.htm

Steele, David. "Back in the Swim: Dara Torres' Remarkable Revival in the Pool Is Making Those Tae-Bo Commercials Ancient History." *San Francisco Chronicle*. August 9, 2000. http://www.sfgate.com/sports/article/Back-in-the-Swim-Dara-Torres-remarkable-3303356.php#page-1

"Steffen Snatches Gold in 50 Free; Torres Takes Silver." Associated Press. August 17, 2008. http://sports.espn.go.com/oly/summer08/swimming/news/story?id=3539007

"Swimmer Kitajima Expects Closer Scrutiny in 200 Breaststroke." *USA Today*. August 18, 2004. http://usatoday30.usatoday.com/sports/olympics/athens/swimming/2004-08-17-kitajima-kick_x.htm?POE=SPOISVA

Tegler, Zach. "Olympic Gold Medalist Pablo Morales Continues to Humbly Lead NU Swimmers." *Daily Nebraskan*. November 27, 2012. http://www.dailynebraskan.com/sports/olympic-gold-medalist-pablo-morales-continues-to-humbly-lead-nu/article_a300ed52-3846-11e2-9724-0019bb30f31a.html

Trucks, Rob. "How a Career Ends: Nancy Hogshead-Makar, Olympic Swimming Gold Medalist." *Deadspin*. July 31, 2012. http://deadspin.com/5930611/how-a-career-ends-nancy-hogshead+makar-olympic-swimming-gold-medalist?src=longreads

Ungerleider, Steven. *Faust's Gold: Inside the East German Doping Machine.* New York: Thomas Dunne Books, 2001.

Weil, Elizabeth. "A Swimmer of a Certain Age." *New York Times.* June 29, 2008. http://www .nytimes.com/2008/06/29/magazine/29torres-t.html?_r=1&oref=slogin&ref=olympics&p agewanted=all

Wright, Sylas. "Golden Moments: Debbie Meyer Talks Olympic Swimming." *Tahoe Daily Tribune.* August 14, 2008. http://www.tahoedailytribune.com/article/20080815/SPORTS/463869672

WEBSITES

fina.org: The official website of the Federation Internationale de Natation, the international governing body for the five aquatic sports: swimming, diving, open-water swimming, water polo, and synchronized swimming.

ishof.org: The official website of the International Swimming Hall of Fame. The website includes biographies of individuals inducted into the hall.

olympic.org: The official website of the International Olympic Committee. The website in-cludes lists of all Olympic medal winners, biographical information on numerous athletes, and details of the Olympic movement.

sports-reference.com: Website with comprehensive historical information on a variety of sports, including a section on the Olympics.

swimming.org.au: The official website of Swimming Australia, the governing body of the sport in Australia. The website includes archived results of national and international com-petition and biographical information on Australian athletes.

swimmingworldmagazine.com: Website of *Swimming World Magazine.* It includes archived articles from magazine issues from 1960 to the present.

swimvortex.com: Based out of Europe, the website provides comprehensive coverage of the sport, including feature writing, column writing, and meet coverage. The website also offers up-to-date world rankings and results.

usaswimming.org: The official website of USA Swimming, the governing body of the sport in the United States. The website includes archived results of national and international competition and biographical information of U.S. athletes.

Index

About the Author

John Lohn is the U.S. correspondent for SwimVortex, supplying the European-based website with meet coverage, feature writing, and column writing on a regular basis. The former senior writer for *Swimming World Magazine*, he has been covering swimming at the elite level for more than a decade, having chronicled the past two Olympic Games, the achievements of Michael Phelps, and every version of the U.S. Olympic Trials since 2000. Additionally, Lohn has covered major events, such as the World Championships, Pan Pacific Championships, U.S. National Championships, and NCAA Championships. Through the years, he has been a guest analyst on several networks, including ESPN and the BBC, and his work has been cited by numerous national and international newspapers and magazines, including *USA Today*, *Bloomberg News*, and the *Christian Science Monitor*, along with media outlets in Australia, Japan, China, Brazil, and Europe. He previously authored *The Historical Dictionary of Competitive Swimming* and *They Ruled the Pool: The 100 Greatest Swimmers in History*, along with providing multiple chapters to *Swimmers: Courage and Triumph*. His work has been award winning—most notably, a 2009 piece on a blind swimmer who competed at the high school level despite his handicap. The article won several newspaper awards and received honorable mention status in the 2010 edition of *The Best American Sports Writing*. A Pennsylvania native and graduate of La Salle University, he resides in New Jersey with his wife, Dana, and their twin daughters, Taylor and Tiernan. He currently works as a media specialist and enjoys fitness training and cruising.